No Nonsense

FLY FISHING GUIDEBOOKS

David
COMMUNICATIONS

Publishers Note: The many contributors to this guidebook deserve our gratitude. They contributed their time and gave us their inside, "secret information" about their favorite fly fishing waters.

The generous folks at SafeWater Anywhere provided an appropriate "thank you". They make a great, lightweight, reliable water bottle that can be filled from any river, stream or lake. Filters in the bottle clean out microorganisms, compounds and industrial waste. With this bottle, one can drink safe water while fly fishing most anywhere.

All contributors to this guidebook received their very own 1/2 LITER PRO Personal Water Filter. Each "Pro" comes with a mesh carrying bag with a pouch for keys and fly fishing gadgets.

Thank you John and Jacquie, and everyone at SafeWater for your great products and for making them available to the female anglers in this guidebook. To contact SafeWater Anywhere call 1-800-675-4401, or visit www.safewateranywhere.com.

A Woman's No Nonsense

Guide To Fly Fishing

Favorite Waters

The Nation's Top Female Fly Fishing Authorities
Give You a Quick, Clear Understanding Of How
to Fly Fish Their Favorite Waters

Published by David Communications • 6171 Tollgate, Sisters, Oregon 97759

A Woman's No Nonsense Guide To Fly Fishing Favorite Waters

Conceived, Compiled & Edited By Yvonne Graham

Additional editing: Jeff Cavender and David Banks. Maps, illustrations and production: Pete & Aprille Chadwell. Published by David Communications, 6171 Tollgate, Sisters, Oregon 97759. Printed by Hignell Book Printing, 488 Burnell Street, Winnipeg, Manitoba, Canada R3G 2B4. Copyright ©2000 David Communications, ISBN #1-892469-03-0.

David Communications believes that in addition to local information and gear, fly fishers need clean water and healthy fish. The publisher encourages preservation, improvement, conservation, enjoyment, and understanding of our waters and their inhabitants. A good way to do this is to support organizations dedicated to these ideas.

David Communications is a member and sponsor of and donor to The International Game Fish Association, Trout Unlimited, The Federation of Fly Fishers, Oregon Trout, California Trout, New Mexico Trout, Amigos Bravos, American Fly-Fishing Trade Association, American Rivers, Waterfowl U.S.A., Ducks Unlimited, and International Women Fly Fishers. We encourage you to get involved, learn more and to join such organizations. IGFA (954) 941-3474, Trout Unlimited 1(800) 834-2419 • Federation of Fly Fishers (406) 585-7592 • Oregon Trout (503) 222-9091 • California Trout (415) 392-8887 • New Mexico Trout (505) 344-6363 • Amigos Bravos (505) 758-3874 • A.F.F.T.A. (360) 636-0708 • American Rivers (202) 547-6900 • Ducks Unlimited (901) 758-3825, IWFF (800)919-2252.

Disclaimer

While this guide will greatly help readers to fly fish, it is not a substitute for caution, good judgement and the services of a qualified fly fishing guide or outfitter.

Acknowledgments

From Yvonne Graham

About 25 years ago, I met and fell in love with the man who was to become my husband, Gary Graham. He introduced me to the sport that was to become our passion. Those two events brought me to this book.

There would be no book, however, if the contributors, my sister anglers, had not enthusiastically said "yes" when I asked them to help me. These very busy women took time out from their endeavors to support me in this project. I thank them wholeheartedly. I am fortunate indeed, to be part of this select sisterhood of women fly fishers. Finally to the publisher, David Banks, who believed in my idea, thank you .

••••

Publishers Note:
This guidebook has many fine contributors. The original idea, the connection with female anglers, the cajoling, and much of the behind the scenes work was entirely that of Yvonne Graham. She has the honor of "Authorship" and the dedication of this guidebook. She is most generous with her acknowledgments as she is with her enthusiasm for fly fishing.

*T*his book is dedicated to my family and friends.
To my husband, Gary: did I ever tell you you're my hero?
To our children: Terri, Julia, Mike and Geoff, to their partners: Stan, Jerry,
Alison and Melody, and to our grandchildren: Lindsey, Josh, Elliott,
Casey, Zane, and Elizabeth. And to my brother, Roger, my almost-sister,
Marnelle, and the many others who are always there for me and who are
"the wind beneath my wings."

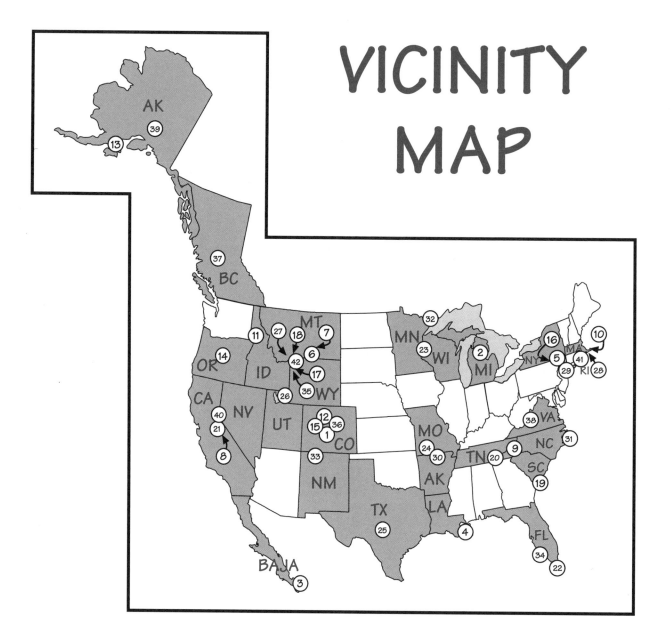

VICINITY MAP

1. ARKANSAS RIVER, CO
2. AU SABLE RIVER, MI
3. BAHIA DE LAS PALMAS, BAJA
4. BARATARIA ESTUARY, LA
5. BEAVERKILL, NY
6. BIG HORN LAKE, MT
7. BIG HORN RIVER, MT
8. BIG PINE CREEK, CA
9. BULLHEAD CREEK, NC
10. CAPE COD, MA
11. CLEARWATER RIVER, ID
12. COLORADO RIVER, CO
13. CONTACT CREEK, AK
14. CROOKED RIVER, OR

15. EAGLE RIVER, CO
16. FERDON'S EDDY, NY
17. FLAT CREEK, WY
18. GALLATIN RIVER, MT
19. HILTON HEAD ISLAND, SC
20. HIWASSEE RIVER, TN
21. HOT CREEK, CA
22. ISLAMORADA, FL
23. KNAPP RIVER, WI
24. LAKE TANEYCOMO, MO
25. LLANO RIVER, TX
26. LOGAN RIVER, UT
27. MADISON RIVER, MT
28. MARTHA'S VINEYARD, MA

29. NEW YORK HARBOR, NY
30. NORFORK RIVER, AK
31. OUTER BANKS, NC
32. POPLAR RIVER, MN
33. SAN JUAN RIVER, NM
34. SANIBEL ISLAND, FL
35. SNAKE RIVER, WY
36. SOUTH PLATTE RIVER, CO
37. STELLAKO RIVER, BC
38. SWEET SPRINGS CREEK, VA
39. TANGLE RIVER, AK
40. TRUCKEE RIVER, NV
41. WOOD RIVER, RI
42. YELLOWSTONE RIVER, WY

Contents

Casting For Recovery

*C*asting For Recovery is a not-for-profit, national organization that puts on retreats for women across the country who are recovering from breast cancer. The CFR goal is to aid their physical, emotional, and spiritual healing.

The weekend retreats are held in beautiful, natural settings where women learn fly fishing: tying a fly, reading water, knot tying, learning about fly fishing gear and casting to fish. The latter activity, the physical act of casting a fly rod, may help reduce swelling and restore mobility which may have been compromised by surgery. Female fly fishing instructors, a therapist, and health care professionals all contribute to the activities.

Fly fishing is a perfect activity for these gatherings for other reasons. Casting For Recovery believes fly fishing, a sport for life, is a window into the natural world and places of solace where emotional healing and well-being flourish. Fly fishing also combines physical activity and intellectual intrigue that creates a sense of accomplishment at day's end. For women whose lives have been profoundly affected by the disease, the emotional benefits, friendships and networking about medical issues at a Casting For Recovery gathering is invaluable and incalculable.

To date, retreats have been held in New York, Pennsylvania, Michigan, Alaska, Maine, Wisconsin, Vermont, and Alberta, Canada. New locations are being added yearly. Casting For Recovery's Board of Advisors include ABC News correspondent Judy Muller and internationally renowned author Dr. Susan Love. The founder and board chair is Gwenn Perkins, and the vice-chair is Margot Page. Casting For Recovery has been covered by *ABC's World News Tonight*, CNN, *The American Medical News*, *The Wall Street Journal* and other magazines and newspapers.

Based in Manchester, Vermont, Casting For Recovery relies entirely on donations to fund their fly fishing retreats. Participants attend without charge. Your purchase of this guidebook contributes to this program. Each CFR participant receives a free copy of this guide. This helps new fly fishers explore special places and fly fishing waters, a perfect way to keep the mind positive and the body active.

For more information about Casting For Recovery or to make a donation please call Program Director, Susan Balch (888-553-3500).

Casting For Recovery Administrative Office
Attention Ms. Seline Skoug PMB 257 • 946 Great Plains Avenue Needham, MA 02492

Dorado

Photo By: Tom Pero

Joan Wulff is an accomplished tournament caster. From 1937 to 1960, she won seventeen national and one international title. In 1978, she established the still very popular Joan and Lee Wulff Fly Fishing Schools as well as, in 1996, the first-ever schools for casting instructors. Since 1980, Joan has written the fly casting column for Fly Rod & Reel *magazine and was the first instructor to analyze the mechanics of fly casting and give names to the parts of the casting stroke in* Joan Wulff's Fly Casting Techniques *(1986). She is also the author of* Fly Casting Accuracy *and a women's angling book,* Joan Wulff's Fly Fishing. *Her recent video,* Dynamics of Fly Casting *is a top seller. She currently works for the R.L. Winston Rod Company.*

Wherever I Am

The Highest Stage Of Fly Fishing
Joan Salvato Wulff

*I*f fly fishing is or is becoming a dominant thread through your life, as it has been in mine, you will go through various stages of involvement with individual species of fish. The first stage is about *numbers* of fish caught, and the second stage is about their size. Then, hopefully, you'll graduate to a third stage, seeking the most *difficult* fish, those that require more of you in approach and presentation, fly selection, and casting prowess. We can be in different stages for different species, depending on how often we fish and our success rate.

In the important fourth stage, you move to a different level and start thinking about *giving* something back to the resource, compelling you to work harder for conservation organizations. But there's even a higher stage, a fifth stage, which I would like to share with you. I call it the *"Just Being There"* stage.

When asked to name my favorite fishing spot or my favorite fish the answer is "wherever I am" or "whatever I'm fishing for" . . . that's stage five!

Game fish live only in clean water . . . in the earth's most beautiful places. And each species, from trout to tarpon, offers special enjoyment, the full appreciation of which can only come with experience. It becomes increasingly difficult to say that one place or species of fish is better than another.

This book is about particular fish in particular stretches of water, each with an abundance of suggestions by skilled anglers that can't help but make it easier to be successful. And I can certainly relate to that.

In my early days of trout fishing, I didn't read water well (despite what you might think, I'm not a natural born fisherman), and I stayed in one spot instead of exploring other sections of the river. Understanding how aquatic insect life related to angling was in its infancy, and my limited fishing knowledge was used up in about two hours of not catching fish. Help, from whatever source, was really appreciated.

Yes, being told where to fish and exactly what flies to use can give you a much-needed helping hand, but you don't want to be on welfare any longer than is absolutely necessary. So don't be afraid to make your own mistakes. In fly fishing as in most aspects of life, independence gives you confidence as well as wonderful highs you'll never experience otherwise.

As a stage five fly fisher, I no longer want guaranteed success. I do want it always to be a challenge, and if I catch three fish on a given fly, I change the fly to see what else the fish might take. Great presentations of odd-ball offerings can and

do catch fish. My late husband Lee could catch trout on dandelion heads and bare hooks when he had or wanted to. A fish can only respond to what you present; you'll never know if a fly will work if it remains in your box. Experiment!

Finally, as I reflect on these words, I think perhaps I've also arrived at a sixth stage: *fishing through others*. My competitive spirit is undergoing change, and I can now enjoy a companion's success as if it were my own. And, because we need continuing generations of anglers to protect the resource, I've become more focused on replacing myself . . . with a youngster.

There's lots for you to look forward to beyond the most and the biggest: just being there, whether you catch fish or not; enjoying the water and the species you are fishing for, wherever or whatever they are; moving away from a sure thing by experimenting with flies; and not caring when you don't remember how many fish you caught. Enjoy it all!

   Fanny Krieger was born in France and came to America when she was seventeen. In Houston, she met and married Mel Krieger, who wanted a business where they could hang out a "Gone Fishing" sign. In the early 1960's, the family moved to San Francisco where Fanny and Mel started Club Pacific, a travel agency for fly fishermen, and began teaching their well-attended fishing schools. A book and three very popular videos soon followed. Fanny is a co-founder of the Golden West Women Fly Fishers. In 1996, with help from club members, she also founded the International Festival of Women Fly Fishers.

My Favorite Fishing Guide

How To Select An Ideal Guide

Fanny Krieger

I am an average fly fisher, and my needs are probably very similar to yours. In choosing a fly fishing guide, I rely primarily on recommendations of other anglers whose opinions I value. In lieu of a first-hand referral, however, I will look to a reputable fly shop or even articles in fly fishing magazines. I recommend you do the same.

My ideal fishing guide could go by the name of Karen or even Mike, no discrimination here. Karen or Mike have been fishing for years and know the local waters well, but most importantly, they are very professional.

Karen picks me up at precisely the time we agreed on when we made our plans the previous day. Her car is clean, and she has extra equipment in case I have forgotten something. When we arrive at our fishing destination, she puts down a carpet and provides a place to sit, so I can put on my waders with some degree of dignity. While I finish my preparations, she puts my rod and reel together and helps me select a fly. As we walk to the river, she makes recommendations and suggestions that will improve my day of fishing, and when we get to the water, she carries my rod while holding my arm to help me wade if the current is too strong.

When I am ready to fish, she carefully explains the pool, the current, and the best presentation. In other words, she guides me through the process of casting to a fish, all the while gently suggesting improvements in my casting and presentation.

After I hook a fish that she realizes I don't have enough experience to handle, Karen will again guide me on the best way to play, land, and safely release it. The experience has been all mine, but she has been the guide.

She does not fish while guiding but does carry an extra rod in case I want to switch from a dry fly to a nymph.

She understands my weaknesses as well as my strengths and will stay quiet when I am comfortable with what is going on. She will not overwhelm me with her knowledge when I am floundering. She has also prepared a nice, restful, streamside lunch and will not push me into more fishing than I wish to do.

Karen is aware that there are times when I want a companion rather than a servant, times when I do not want advice, and times when I would prefer to fish alone, choosing my own flies and fishing independently.

Obviously, Karen is a bit of a psychologist and philosopher as well as being a very fine angler. She is good company without being pushy, and, over the course of our time spent together, she has also become a friend. I will fish with her again.

Follow the above guidelines when choosing a fly fishing guide anywhere in the world. In doing so, I hope you will be fortunate enough to find your own Karen or Mike. Happily, they do exist.

Largemouth Bass.

Women's Favorite Fly Fishing Waters

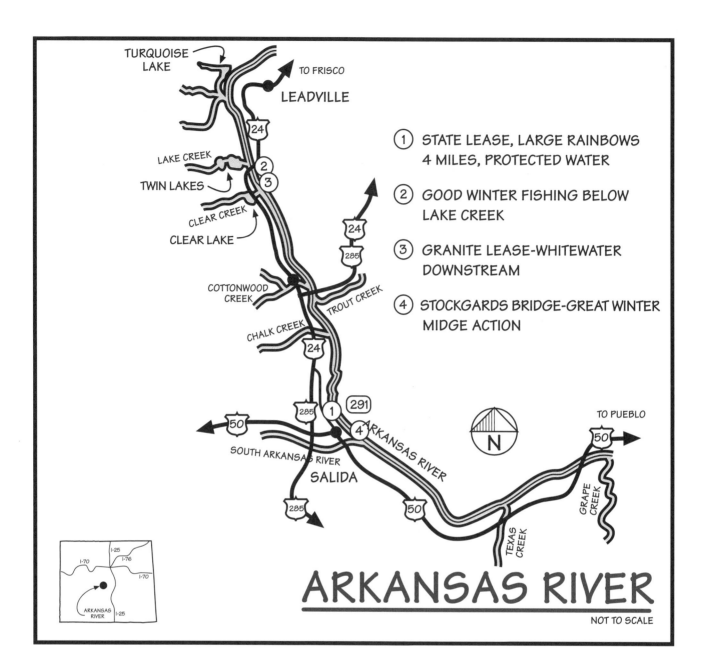

TURQUOISE LAKE

TO FRISCO

LEADVILLE

24

LAKE CREEK

2

TWIN LAKES

3

CLEAR CREEK

CLEAR LAKE

24

285

COTTONWOOD CREEK

TROUT CREEK

CHALK CREEK

24

291

285

1

50

4

ARKANSAS RIVER

SOUTH ARKANSAS RIVER

N

TO PUEBLO

50

SALIDA

285

50

TEXAS CREEK

GRAPE CREEK

1. STATE LEASE, LARGE RAINBOWS 4 MILES, PROTECTED WATER

2. GOOD WINTER FISHING BELOW LAKE CREEK

3. GRANITE LEASE-WHITEWATER DOWNSTREAM

4. STOCKGARDS BRIDGE-GREAT WINTER MIDGE ACTION

I-70 I-25 I-76 I-70 I-25

ARKANSAS RIVER

ARKANSAS RIVER

NOT TO SCALE

B. J. Lester is a fishing guide and family counselor and recognizes the therapeutic value inherent in her two vocations, both for herself and for her clients. Fly fishing has been a part of B.J.'s life since she was ten when her uncle taught her to cast to big bass in Mississippi and Louisiana. In 1989, she started tying flies, an activity that has since become the major focus of her fly fishing experience. In addition to her counseling practice in Lyons, Colorado, B.J. guides for Brower's Fly Shop on the Arkansas, teaches casting and tying for various shops, gives tying demonstrations at sportsmen's shows and other events, and serves on the pro staff for several fly tackle manufacturers.

Arkansas River
Colorado
B.J. Lester

A short two-and-one-half hours from Denver, Colorado, anglers will discover not only the majestic peaks, red cliffs, and deep canyons of one of the most beautiful valleys in the state, but also a gem of a trout fishery. Fed by the snow melt of the massive Collegiate Range that surrounds the valley, the Arkansas River tumbles 120 miles between Leadville and Canon City. After a runoff period that typically starts in late May and often varies in duration and intensity depending on the snow pack, the Arkansas River settles down to the pocket water, deep pools, and riffles of a typical, Rocky Mountain, freestone stream. The river boasts approximately 3,000 trout per mile which average between 11-14 inches, and the fly fishing can range from "too easy" to extremely difficult, especially considering the variety of water encountered on the Arkansas as well as its year-round season.

While dry fly fishing is best from May through September, the Arkansas River is most famous for its "Mother's Day Caddis Hatch." Envision a gray cloud of insects hanging over the water, and caddis covering the legs of your waders and swarming so thickly around your face that it seems difficult to see or even breath. Picture also lots of hungry trout sipping bugs, their noses poking through the surface as they break a long winter's fast, and you get some idea of why this phenomenal hatch attracts anglers from all over the western United States.

As you might imagine, caddis patterns are especially effective mid-April through June, and Baetis patterns are important throughout the warmer months. Nymph fishing, of course, is always effective on the Arkansas, and don't forget to bring along an assortment of streamers.

Type of Fish
Brown and rainbow trout.

Known Hatches or Baitfish
March - July, Sept. - October: Baetis
April - June, Mid July - September: Caddis
June - August: Golden Stones and Little Yellow Sallies
July - September: Pale Morning Duns and Red Quills
Year round: Midges

Equipment to Use
Rods: 9 foot, 4 to 6 weight.
Reels: Disk or click to match rod, 100 yds. 20 lb. backing.
Lines: Weight forward or double taper to match rod.
Leaders: Typically 9 foot, 4 to 7X.
Wading or Boating: Breathable or neoprene waders, felt soled boots. Boating very technical. Best to use a guide service.

Flies to Use
Dries: January-April, Griffith's Gnat, midge emerger, Palomino midge #18-22. March-June and Sept.-Dec., Adams #14-22, parachute Baetis #20-22, Sparkle Dun #16-20, AK's Olive Quill #16-12. April - mid-June, dark gray Elk Hair Caddis, Marty's Bead Butt Egg Laying Caddis, peacock body fluttering caddis #16-18. Mid-May - July, Stimulator #8 -12, Kaufmann's Golden Stone #6-12. June-Sept., PMD, Sparkle

Dun #14-18, Royal Wulff, Humpy #10-16, AK's Hopper #8-12, Black Ant #14-20.
Nymphs: Hare's Ears #10-16, Buckskin, Pheasant Tail #16-20, Sparkle Caddis Pupa #10-20, Black Beauty #18-24, Brassie #16-24, Palomino Midge #18-22, Golden Stone #8-10, Bread Crust #12-16, Theo's Danger Baby #12-16.
Streamers: Muddler Minnow #4-10, Spruce #8-12, Woolly Bugger, Black Nose Dace #6-12.

When to Fish
The best fishing is May through October.

Seasons & Limits
Open year-round, artificial flies and lures only, limit 2 fish, 16" or over.

Accommodations & Services
Motels, gas, food and fly shops in Buena Vista and Salida.

Nearby Fly Fishing
South Platte, Gunnison and Taylor Rivers, Chalk Creek, and unlimited backcountry fly fishing opportunities.

Rating
Good weather, great scenery, plenty of public water, and lots of trout, the Arkansas River deserves a solid 8.

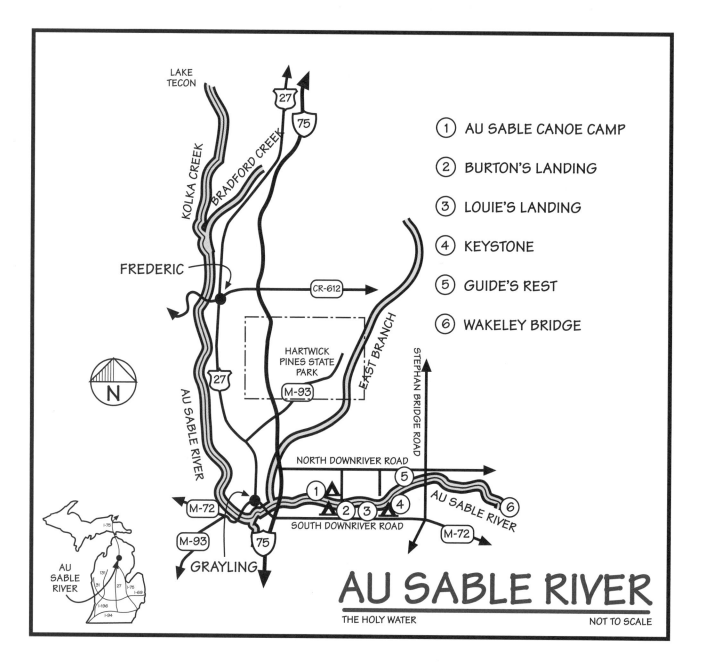

LAKE TECON

KOLKA CREEK

BRADFORD CREEK

27

75

① AU SABLE CANOE CAMP

② BURTON'S LANDING

③ LOUIE'S LANDING

④ KEYSTONE

⑤ GUIDE'S REST

⑥ WAKELEY BRIDGE

FREDERIC

CR-612

N

HARTWICK PINES STATE PARK

EAST BRANCH

M-93

27

AU SABLE RIVER

STEPHAN BRIDGE ROAD

NORTH DOWNRIVER ROAD

⑤

M-72

①

② ③ ④

⑥

AU SABLE RIVER

SOUTH DOWNRIVER ROAD

M-93

75

M-72

GRAYLING

AU SABLE RIVER

I-75

131

31

27

I-75

I-69

I-196

I-94

AU SABLE RIVER

THE HOLY WATER

NOT TO SCALE

Connie Geurink is Associate Producer of Outdoor Adventures, *a national television show that promotes women and children's involvement in the outdoors. She has filmed, hunted and fished throughout North America, including the U.S., Canada, and Mexico. Connie also guides ladies hunting trips to Russia, primarily in the Crimea on the shores of the Black Sea. She has published hunting and fishing articles in several Michigan newspapers and magazines and is a member of the Women in the Outdoors Program, Michigan United Conservation Club's North Country Trail Association, Women's Shooting Sports Foundation, and Michigan Outdoor Women's Club.*

Au Sable River
Michigan
The "Holy Water"
Connie Geurink

Michigan is a fly fisher's paradise, and choosing just one destination is no small task. But one location in particular is just about perfect—the Au Sable River, rated as one of this country's top ten, "Blue Ribbon" trout streams.

It's a short drive from Grayling, Michigan to the Michigan stretch of water between Burton's Landing and Wakeley Bridge known as the "Holy Water." Designated as "fly only" water and chock full of rainbows, browns, and brookies, this famous section of the Au Sable is known as much for the diversity of its hatches as it is for its wild and scenic beauty. And, while it does have swift riffles and deep pools, the river's gravel bottom and long stretches of clear, shallow water make it perfect for wading. Take all of the above and combine it with the fact that the "Holy Water" section is open all year, and you end up with some truly world class trout fishing.

One of the best places to start fishing this wonderful stretch of river is at Gates Au Sable Lodge. Take I-75 to Grayling then M-72 east seven miles to Stephan Bridge Road. Turn left and go north two miles to the lodge. There, you will find a complete Orvis Pro Shop, along with lodging and an excellent restaurant. The lodge is open April through October, and owner, Rusty Gates, will be happy to provide guide service and help with any questions. He can be contacted at 517-348-8462.

For more information on the Au Sable and its tributaries, contact the Fisheries Division, MDNR, by mail at P.O. Box 30446, Lansing, MI 48909 or by phone at 571-826-3211. You can also visit their web site at www.dnr.state.mi.us. Another great source of information, with lots of details, maps, etc., is Tom Huggler's guide book, *"Fish Michigan" 50 Rivers*. For a copy, contact Tom at 800-735-3476 or send $20.95 to Outdoor Images, P.O. Box 250, Sunfield, MI 48890.

Type of Fish
Rainbows, browns, and brookies.

Equipment to Use
Rods: 9 foot, 4 to 5 weight.
Reels: Disc or click to match rod with 50 to 100 yards of 20 pound backing.
Lines: Weight forward or double taper, floating to match rod.
Leaders: Typically 9 foot, 4 to 7X.
Wading: Very wadeable using breathable or neoprene waders and felt soled boots.

Flies to Use
Black or brown caddis, sulfur dun #14-16, hendrickson, red or black quill #12-14, brown or gray drake #8-10, blue dun #16-18, blue winged olive dun #18-20.

When to Fish
Spring with its big hatches and fall are the best times.

Seasons & Limits
The season is open year-round. Fly only.

Accommodations & Services
You'll find plenty of easy access points along the river as well as several campgrounds. There are motels available in nearby Grayling. For more information about accommodations, call the Grayling Chamber of Commerce at 517-348-2921.

Nearby Fly Fishing
Michigan is a fly angler's paradise with many lakes and streams full of trout.

Rating
This fabled water is definitely a 10.

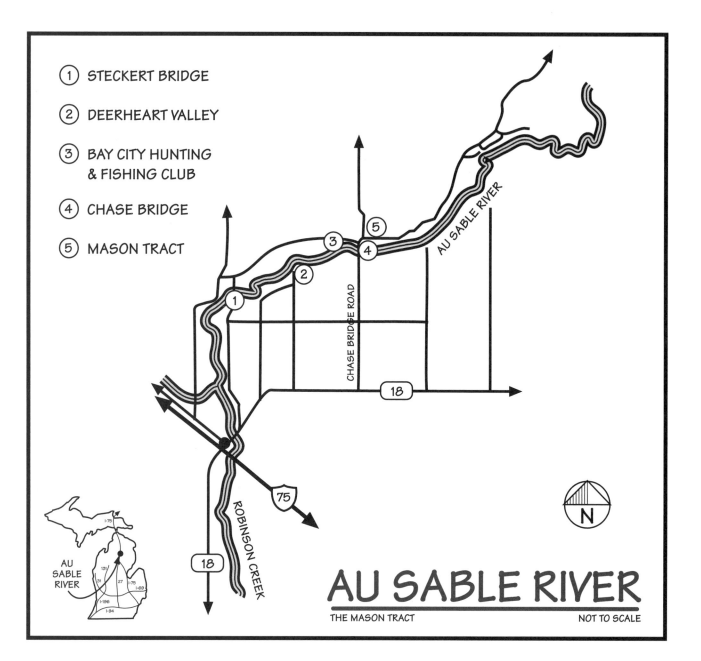

1. STECKERT BRIDGE
2. DEERHEART VALLEY
3. BAY CITY HUNTING & FISHING CLUB
4. CHASE BRIDGE
5. MASON TRACT

AU SABLE RIVER

THE MASON TRACT

NOT TO SCALE

Dorothy Schramm is the owner of Rodsmith, a custom rod building and angling related arts business with customers in thirty-eight states and several foreign countries. She is a Federation Of Fly Fishers Certified Casting Instructor, a demonstration fly tier, current Vice President of Women's Education for the FFF, and the 1998 recipient of the Woman of the Year award. Dorothy lives in Pentwater, Michigan with her husband, Jim, an environmental attorney. When she is not over the top of her waders in volunteer work for the resource, you can usually find her on the Pere Marquette River listening for the heartbeats of steelhead.

Au Sable River
Michigan
The Mason Tract
Dorothy Schramm

*L*ocated near Grayling, Michigan, the Mason Tract of the Au Sable consists of 1,200 acres that enclose both banks of the South Branch of this famed river system. This section of the river is named for George Mason, the man who encouraged George Griffith to form Trout Unlimited. Mason left this property to the State of Michigan to be held in perpetuity in its natural state. Upon entering the Mason Tract from Chase Bridge Road, you pass a sign saying, "Sportsmen slow your pace … ahead lies the fabled land of the South Branch. Here generations of fishermen have cast a fly on one of the great trout streams of America. Hunters, too, have roamed these hills in the solitude so bountifully offered. The land is rich in tradition and stands ready to renew your soul. Tread lightly as you pass and leave no mark. Go forth in the spirit of George W. Mason whose generous gift has made this forever possible."

The Au Sable River as it flows through the Mason Tract ranges from 20 to 40' wide and from 1 to 6' or more deep. This is classic trout water, gently meandering through pristine pine forests and swamps, shaded by overhanging cedars and crisscrossed with shoreline dead falls which seem to form bridges across time. Occasional small islands, lush with wild flowers, greet the wading angler who explores the stream's many pools, riffles and log jams. Here, even with well-marked paths and spread-out parking clearings, you get a sense of wilderness.

The Au Sable River flows through the Mason Tract at a soothing pace, gently surrounding an angler with a sense of history and mystery. You can almost hear the casts of every angler who ever fished here before and who also cared for this river. Great blue herons and kingfishers will accompany you on your hunt, honorable fishing partners to say the least.

Reaching the Mason Tract is relatively simple. Four-wheel-drive is not necessary, but the road off Chase Bridge Road, north off of 18 out of Roscommon, is a sand two track. Sometimes dead falls block the road, and you should be well familiar with exits points along the river before attempting to leave after dark.

Types of Fish
Trophy browns, brookies, and the occasional rainbow.

Known Hatches
Black and tan caddis, gray drakes, Hexagenias, blue winged olives, little yellow stones, damselflies, and terrestrials

Equipment to Use
Rods: 7 to 9 foot, 3 to 5 weight.
Reels: To balance rod. A smooth drag is preferable.
Lines: Floating, weight forward or double taper to match rod.
Leaders: 7 to 10', 3X for big streamers, 6X for small flies.
Wading & boating: Wading preserves the pristine experience, but the river can be canoed. A float trip takes 8 to 10 hours.

Flies to Use
Dries: Hexagenia duns & spinners, Elk Hair & CDC Caddis, Adams, Spentwing Adams, Little Yellow Stones, Skunks, Mattress Thrashers, Patriots, hoppers, damsel flies, ants, inchworms.
Nymphs: Hexagenia emergers, Pheasant Tails, damsel flies.

Streamers: October Fly, Pass Lakes, large weighted, olive (white after dark) marabou streamers.

When to Fish
Any time of day, but evenings are best for big fish.

Seasons & Limits
Last Saturday in April to October 31st. From Chase Bridge to lower High Banks, artificial flies, catch and release only.

Accommodations & Services
Gate's Au Sable Lodge has restaurant, fly shop. In Grayling, The Fly Factory shop and motels, campgrounds, and services.

Nearby Fishing
Au Sable Mainstream, Wakeley Lake (panfish, pike, bass), Neff Lake (trout), and the Manistee River.

Rating
Various hatches and size of quarry, a strong 8.

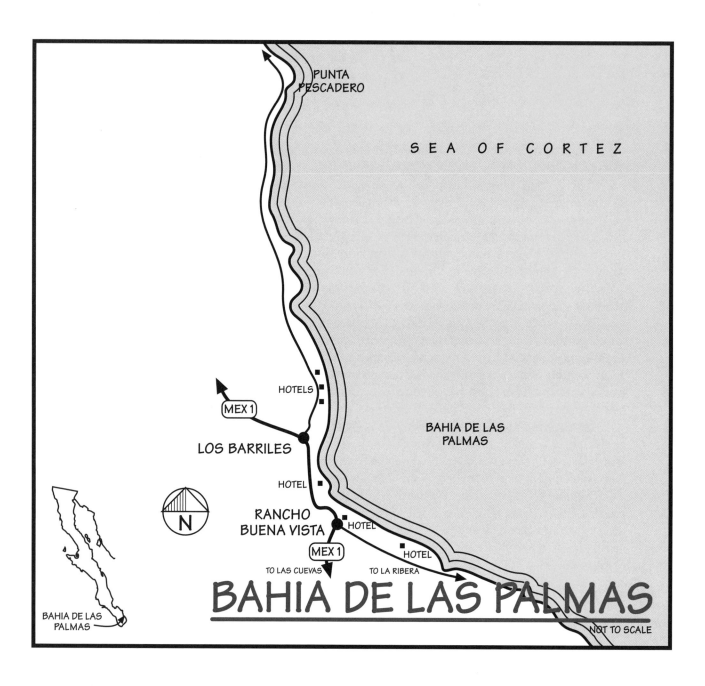

PUNTA
PESCADERO

SEA OF CORTEZ

HOTELS

MEX 1

BAHIA DE LAS
PALMAS

LOS BARRILES

HOTEL

N

RANCHO
BUENA VISTA   HOTEL

MEX 1

TO LAS CUEVAS   TO LA RIBERA   HOTEL

BAHIA DE LAS
PALMAS

BAHIA DE LAS PALMAS

NOT TO SCALE

Yvonne Watson-Graham became the first woman to catch a striped marlin on both 8 and 12 pound test in the same season. She is also a three-time, IGFA, world record holder, twice receiving the coveted 10-to-1 Award. In the early 80's, Yvonne and her husband Gary, were co-directors of the National Coalition of Marine Conservation, West Coast. They also established the Friends of Fishing Foundation, introducing underprivileged children to sport fishing, and their work with the Big Brothers/Big Sisters Organization became the model for similar fishing programs throughout the country. Yvonne is a Director of the International Festival of Women Fly Fishers. She and Gary currently operate an Orvis-endorsed expedition company, Baja on the Fly.

Bahia Las Palmas
Southern Baja
Yvonne Graham

When you arrive in Baja, you step back in time about 25 years, to a time and place where the pace is slow and the people are friendly and eager to please. The sun almost always shines, and *cerveza* and margaritas flow at night while fishing stories are swapped.

Baja's Sea of Cortez, often called a fisherman's paradise, boasts many areas for the saltwater flyrodder. My favorite place is *Bahia Las Palmas* or Bay of Palms. Here, the emerald-green water is calm almost all year round, its temperature never colder than sixty-five or higher than ninety. Although there are reportedly 850 species of fish in the Sea of Cortez, you will probably be casting from the beach to a variety of five or six of these fish.

To fish this area, make a reservation at one of the local "flyrod friendly" hotels listed below. To reach most of the hotels, fly into the *Los Cabos* Airport and take Mexico Highway One. The turnoffs to the hotels are consecutive and signed after Kilometer 103. For *Punta Colorado*, turn off at *La Rivera* (before you arrive at K 103) and follow the signs to the hotel. The employees of the hotels speak English, and the area is safe and comfortable for people who are traveling alone.

The miles of beaches that connect the hotels offer great fishing and are my favorite areas to fish with a fly rod. In the silence of the early morning, you can hear the bait fish breaking the surface. Spectacular sunrises often bring birds looking for breakfast. Watch these friends, they help you locate your prey.

Mid-morning, the sun is bright enough for you to see into the clear water and watch fish swim lazily along the beach. You are also close enough to your hotel to find shade or take a midday *siesta*. This accomplished, you are near enough to the water to arise, walk fifty yards or so, and fish some more. This is a fly fishing pace and convenience that should be experienced as often as possible.

Types of Fish
Roosterfish, jack crevalle, ladyfish, pargo, needlefish, pompano, trumpet fish (cornet fish), and sierra.

Equipment to Use
Rods: 9 foot, 8 or 9 weight.
Reels: Direct drive or anti-reverse, disc drag designed for saltwater with quick take-apart, easy clean feature.
Lines: 350 grain full fly line or shooting head and intermediate sink or sink-tip.
Leaders: 6 foot, 20 pound, non-tapered mono. Short wire tippet for Sierra.
Other: Polarized sunglasses a must! Stripping basket and foot protection.
Wading or Boating: Wet wade with booties or sandals. Float tubes or small inflatable pontoon boats. Some of the hotels rent kayaks. The local hotels charter boats.

Flies to Use
Clousers and Deceivers in white, gray, grown, blue, yellow or green (use plenty of flash). Gary's La Rubia in white or green, and Popovic's Surf Candy in blue, green or white.

When to Fish
Generally fishing is best in the spring and summer. All day is wonderful, but early morning (graylight) can be very productive. After about 10:00 a.m., you can usually spot the fish swimming close to shore.

Accommodations & Services
Numerous "flyrod friendly" hotels in the vicinity including *Hotel Buena Vista Beach Resort*, *Rancho Buena Vista*, *Hotel Rancho Leonero*, *Las Palmas*, *Playa de Oro*, and *Punta Colorado*. All are located right on the beach. There are several restaurants and markets as well as beach camping.

Nearby Fly Fishing
The entire shoreline offers good fishing at various times of the day. Many of the skippers and deckhands have experience with fly anglers. From boats, target dorado, rooster, bonito, skipjack, marlin, sailfish, tuna, wahoo, and shore fish.

Rating
Some of the finest fishing in the world and the thrill of a real Mexican adventure, definitely a 10.

9

LAKE PONTCHARTRAIN

TO I-12

TO BATON
ROUGE

NEW ORLEANS

10

90

10

610

61

10

TO HOUMA

90

90

23

BELLE CHASSE

MISSISSIPPI RIVER

LAKE
CATOUATCHIE

LAKE
SALVADOR

I-20

I-49

I-12

I-10

BARATARIA
ESTUARY

N

23

MYRTLE GROVE

TO THE
GULF OF
MEXICO

BARATARIA ESTUARY

NOT TO SCALE

Rebecca S. Rudnick teaches law at schools throughout the United States, usually taking along a fly rod wherever she travels. In addition to fly fishing for redfish along the Gulf Coast, she has fished the saltwaters of Florida, Honduras, and Mexico. Her fishing has also taken her to the Republic of Palau as well as to the steelhead rivers of the Pacific Northwest. Rebecca makes her psychological home with her spouse, Robert Anthoine, in New York City. While teaching at Tulane she discovered the Barataria Estuary in Louisiana through the help of Susan Gros of New Orleans, who has caught several world record redfish on a fly rod.

Barataria Estuary
Louisiana
Rebecca S. Rudnick

*T*ired of wandering the French Quarter? Had enough of Mardi Gras or the Jazz Festival? Are you attending a convention in New Orleans and find yourself in need of a break? Well, if you love great redfishing, the Barataria Estuary in Myrtle Grove is the place to head. A mere thirty-five minutes from the Mississippi River Bridge in downtown New Orleans, the marshes and live oak-lined waterways beckon with great fishing and solitude.

The Barataria Estuary is a bird-watcher's delight with great blue herons, snowy and cattle egrets, ducks, cormorants, and brown pelicans, but it is also home to redfish, averaging four to five pounds. Flanked by live oak, the access from Wood Park to Myrtle Grove Marinas is lined with fishing camps and small communities. The actual fishing waters of the estuary, however, are undisturbed by the sight of human habitation other than an occasional abandoned or working shrimp boat and discreet evidence of oil and gas exploration.

The area is best fished with a guide and from low-draft, flats or john boats with Go Devil engines. I recommend Captains Mark Brockhoeft and Bubby Rodriguez (Big Red Guides and Outfitters, New Orleans) and Kirby LaCour (BKD Guide Service, Kenner).

The techniques used for redfish are very similar to those used for bonefish. Casts need not be particularly long, and the fly is retrieved with a steady strip. When a redfish strikes, you'll need to set the hook with a pull from the retrieving hand rather than raising the rod.

From New Orleans, take Highway 90 W crossing the Mississippi River Bridge to the Westbank. Exit #7, Lafayette Street. Make a left onto Belle Chasse Highway (#23) towards Belle Chasse going through the Belle Chasse tunnel to Myrtle Grove Marina. Highway 23 follows the Mississippi River on the left and Barataria Estuary on the right. The marina is on an access road on the right of Highway 23 in Myrtle Grove. There is also the private Wood Park Marina in Myrtle Grove on the right side of the highway.

Types of Fish
Redfish, speckled trout, sheepshead, black drum, large mouth bass, occasionally flounder.

Equipment to Use
Rods: 9 foot, 7 to 9 weight.
Reels: Direct or anti-reverse model for salt water with disc drag system and quick take-apart for cleaning.
Lines: Full floating fly line preferably with bass or bonefish weight forward taper for wind and distance or an appropriate shooting head system. Winter months redfish go to deeper water, use intermediate or sink-tip lines.
Leaders: 6 foot tapered mono. Start with 16 lb.
Boating: No wading or tubing the muddy bottom shallows. Low draft boat required. Shore fishing at the Myrtle Grove Marina. *Other:* Polarized sunglasses, insect repellant, sun screen, rain jacket, hat.

Flies to Use
Blue crab patterns mimicking redfish's staple diet. Most common flies used, gold and red weedless spoon, brown and red bendback, Clouser, and blue and silver popper.

When to Fish
Redfish are line shy. Low light better than bright light. First 3 hours in a.m. seem to be best. Redfish most aggressive mid-April to mid-June and mid-October to mid-November, all day. South wind or no wind is best, west wind is generally to be avoided. Outgoing tides seem to produce better action.

Seasons & Limits
Fish year-round. Five fish per person per day including one over 27". All fish must be at least 16" long.

Accommodations & Services
Several service stations and food marts on Highway 23. Hotels and motels from elegant to passable in New Orleans, Gretna, and Metarie. In Belle Chasse I recommend Salvo's Seafood and Deli and Ben Becnel's Southern Louisiana Citrus Farm stand.

Rating
Because of the quality of the fishing and its proximity to New Orleans, this area is a 9 for inshore fishing for redfish.

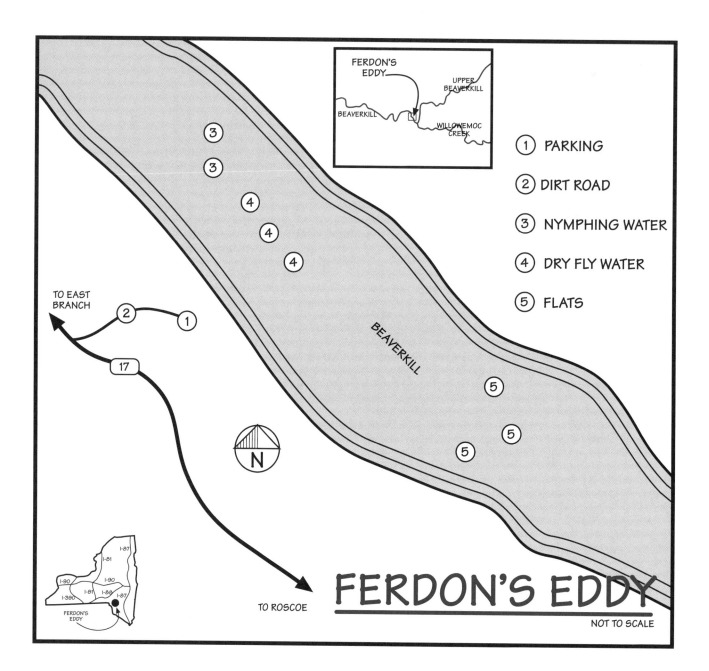

FERDON'S EDDY

UPPER BEAVERKILL

BEAVERKILL

WILLOWEMOC CREEK

① PARKING

② DIRT ROAD

③ NYMPHING WATER

④ DRY FLY WATER

⑤ FLATS

TO EAST BRANCH

BEAVERKILL

N

TO ROSCOE

FERDON'S EDDY

NOT TO SCALE

FERDON'S EDDY

Mary Dette Clark is the daughter of the legendary fly tiers Winnie and Walt Dette of Roscoe, New York. Raised by fly fishing and tying parents on the famed Beaverkill and Willowemoc Rivers, Mary enjoyed a storybook introduction into the fly fishing industry. She has been commercially tying for over forty-four years. Today (unfortunately she says), she does much more tying than fishing although she still enjoys getting out to cast a fly when she gets a chance.

Beaverkill River
New York
Mary Dette Clark

My family history has a lot to do with one of my favorite fishing spots. My mother was raised at the Ferdon's Riverview Inn right on the Beaverkill River where fly fishermen have been congregating since the turn of the century.

Surrounded by beautiful scenery, Ferdon's Pool is located on Old Rt. 17, going west out of Roscoe, New York. You'll go over a bridge that crosses the Beaverkill River just outside of town and then around a big curve. Near the end of the curve is a state fishing sign and a dirt road. Taking a sharp left, this road will take you down to a parking area by the river. The quality of the fishing on this section of the Beaverkill as well as its accessibility, including handicapped and wheelchair access, make this a favorite stop for fly anglers from all over the world who have come to wet their lines in this legendary river.

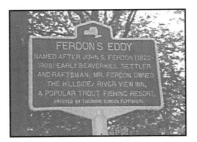

Types of Fish
Brown trout.

Known Hatches
Quill gordons, hendricksons, march browns, gray foxes, drakes, large blue winged olives, cahills, sulphurs, Baetis, caddis, terrestrials and midges.

Equipment to Use
Rods: 9 foot, 4 to 6 weight.
Reels: Disc or click to match rod, 50 to 100 yards of 20 lb. backing.
Lines: Weight forward or double taper floating, in weight to match rod.
Leaders: Typically 9 foot, 4 to 7X.
Wading: Easy wading, wear lightweight waders and boots.

Flies to Use
Dries: Flies that are hatching, including quill gordons, hendricksons, march browns, gray foxes, gray drakes, large blue winged olives, cahills, sulphurs, Baetis, caddis, terrestrials and midges.
Nymphs: Stones, Isonychias, Hare's Ears, and what is hatching at the time.
Streamers: Wooly Buggers and the usual array.

When to Fish
The season opens April 1st, but the best fishing doesn't start until late April continuing into May and June.

Season & Limits
April 1st to the end of September or October on the "open" water. The "No Kill" areas are open all year.

Accommodations & Services
Restaurants, motels, campgrounds, fishing stores are available nearby.

Nearby Fly Fishing
Many other fly fishing areas such as the Delaware River System are very close.

Rating
At the risk of sounding biased, for history, accessibility and setting, a 10 during the late spring and early summer. A century's worth of fly anglers can't be wrong.

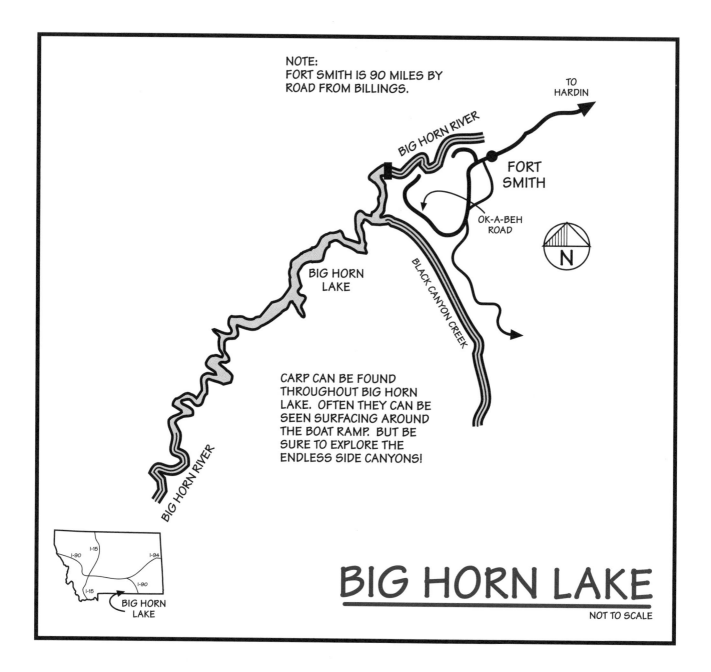

NOTE:
FORT SMITH IS 90 MILES BY
ROAD FROM BILLINGS.

TO HARDIN

BIG HORN RIVER

FORT SMITH

OK-A-BEH ROAD

N

BIG HORN LAKE

BLACK CANYON CREEK

CARP CAN BE FOUND
THROUGHOUT BIG HORN
LAKE. OFTEN THEY CAN BE
SEEN SURFACING AROUND
THE BOAT RAMP. BUT BE
SURE TO EXPLORE THE
ENDLESS SIDE CANYONS!

BIG HORN RIVER

I-15
I-90
I-94
I-15
I-90

BIG HORN
LAKE

BIG HORN LAKE

NOT TO SCALE

Kim Keeley has guided for the last seven years in Idaho, Montana, and Wyoming. Currently, she works for Reel Women Outfitters as a fly fishing guide, lead instructor, and trip leader. Kim also serves as a member of the Powell Rod Company's Factory Team and travels the world introducing women and men to the sport of fly fishing, both in fresh and saltwater. The Tequeely, a streamer of Kim's design, is featured in the Orvis catalog and was listed by Sports Afield *Magazine as a hot new fly in 1998.*

Big Horn Lake
Montana
Kim Keeley

*P*icture a five-pound fish cruising slowly, fifty feet in front of you. You make a perfect cast, placing your dry fly gently on the water just inches from its nose. Slowly, the fish rises and engulfs the fly. Wait...Wait...Wait some more. Now, set the hook...*CARP ON*!

Needless to say, carp fishing does not have the romantic allure and expectations of beautiful scenery associated with trout fishing. In fact, even the mention of fishing for carp in a group of serious fly anglers is typically rewarded with sharp snorts followed by laughter. But, in this age of increasing pressure on our favorite fishing waters, branching out to nontraditional species often provides the solitude we all seek. Big Horn Lake offers this solitude coupled with the challenge of hooking one of the toughest gamefish—yes, gamefish—in the world.

When casting to carp, technique is crucial and quite different from what the average fly angler might be used to. Once a carp has been sighted (look for cruisers just below the surface or a telltale crescent of rubbery lips sucking the surface scum), the cast must be precise and delicate and no more than eighteen inches in front of the fish. If the carp appears to miss or refuse the fly, be patient. More often than not, the fish will turn around and hit again. When the fish takes the fly, WAIT before setting the hook. This is crucial! Once the carp has come down over the fly and re-submerged, then set the hook and hold on. Don't be surprised when your backing shoots through the top guide; carp are tremendously strong fish.

If the carp are not "rising," try a nymph dropper about eighteen inches below your dry fly. The water is clear enough that you'll be able to see the fish eat the nymph. Again, it's crucial to wait for the fly to fully disappear before setting the hook.

One final note: the local tradition is to kiss the first carp you land in order to assure future fishing success!

Types of Fish
Carp, rainbow and brown trout, crappie, smallmouth bass, walleye.

Known Hatches
Algae.

Equipment to Use
Rods: 9 foot, 4 to 7 weight.
Reels: Click or disc drag to balance rod.
Lines: Weight forward or double taper, floating.
Leaders: 9 to 12 foot, 3X.
Wading or Boating: Fishing is from drift boats or similar craft. A saltwater flats boat rigged with a small trolling motor would be perfect.

Flies to Use
Big attractor dry flies like hoppers, Royal Wulff, Yellow Humpies, often with nymph droppers like scuds, beadhead Hare's Ears, Zug Bugs, and Prince Nymphs.

When to Fish
Best April to November except in June when the carp spawn. Spring usually arrives in late May, and the wildflowers are spectacular! Mid-July is the annual Big Lips Tournament.

Seasons & Limits
Open year round. $5.00 daily fee for Big Horn Lake.

Accommodations & Services
Ft. Smith has several motels, lodges and camping facilities as well as a general store, restaurant, and fly shops with guide services. Book well in advance due to the popularity of the area.

Nearby Fly Fishing
When your arms tire from battling big carp, head to the world famous Big Horn River for a little trout fishing.

Rating
The challenge of hooking carp on a dry fly combined with the inspiring scenery surrounding Big Horn Lake make this experience a 9.

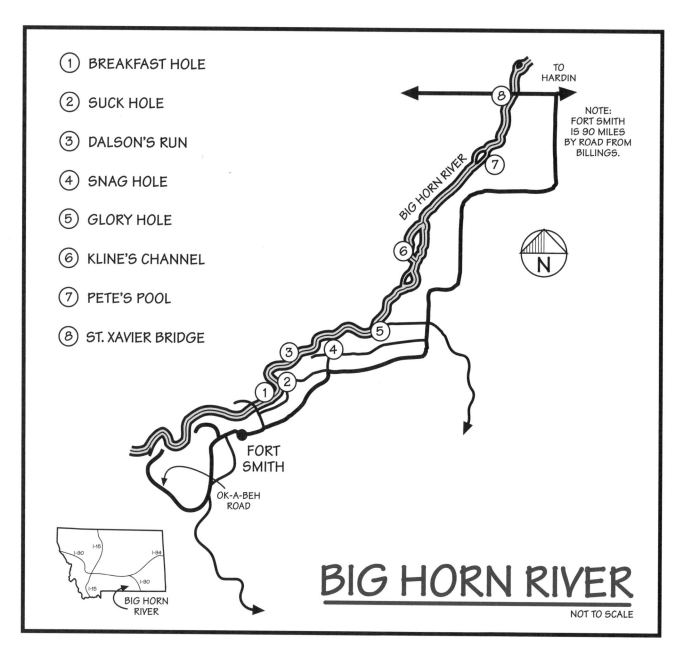

1. BREAKFAST HOLE
2. SUCK HOLE
3. DALSON'S RUN
4. SNAG HOLE
5. GLORY HOLE
6. KLINE'S CHANNEL
7. PETE'S POOL
8. ST. XAVIER BRIDGE

TO HARDIN

NOTE:
FORT SMITH
IS 90 MILES
BY ROAD FROM
BILLINGS.

BIG HORN RIVER

N

FORT SMITH

OK-A-BEH ROAD

I-90 I-15 I-94 I-90 I-15

BIG HORN RIVER

BIG HORN RIVER

NOT TO SCALE

Nancy Zakon loves fly fishing—teaching it, talking it and organizing women's fishing clubs that share the sport with others. An experienced angler, she is on the Orvis Advisory Team. She taught in Orvis' first women's schools and helped design their first technical clothing for women. An FFF Certified Casting Instructor, Nancy graduated from Joan Wulff's Instructors School. She founded the Juliana Berners' Anglers of New York and served on the Interim Steering Committee of the new International Women Fly Fishers. Her publications include The Juliana, *a bi-monthly, women's fishing newsletter. Nancy has appeared in* Fortune, Outdoor Life, Fly Rod & Reel *magazines and Lyla Foggia's book,* Reel Women.

Big Horn River
Montana
Nancy Zakon

*T*en thousand trout per mile ... more than triple that of most rivers! The first time I heard that about the Big Horn River in eastern Montana, I didn't believe it. It also sounded very remote, a long way from the more familiar Livingston/Ennis areas and the Yellowstone and Madison. But I finally tried this much talked about river, and now I prefer it over my old fishing haunts.

The Big Horn River at Ft. Smith is inside the Crow Indian Reservation about eighty-five miles southeast of Billings. Although it's a thirteen-mile tailwater flowing north through the Big Horn Mountains, some refer to it as a huge spring creek due to its unbelievable trout population.

Putting in below Yellowstone Dam on my first day, I witnessed an early morning hatch of blue winged olives swarming up river. My guide stopped the boat just downstream from the dam, so I could wade the far side where fish were feeding everywhere. Quietly, my guide said, "They let you be here." I kept this thought with me as I landed and released my first lovely, big brown. That day, I released many more trout, some going eighteen to twenty inches, and lost a few even larger.

Although I fished a dry fly exclusively that first day, I saw many more boats whose anglers were nymph fishing. I recommend that you brush up on your nymphing technique if you want to increase your fish landing odds.

As an added attraction, you might want to visit the Little Big Horn battlefield which is only thirty miles southwest of Ft. Smith. If you're there in late summer, the Crow Indian Fair is a must with many crafts and foods as well as a rodeo.

The Big Horn River is about 90 minutes drive from the Billings airport. Go east on Interstate 90 out of Billings until you reach the Hardin exit. Turn south on Highway 313, which goes through Xavier, and then take a left at the Ft. Smith/Yellowstone Dam sign.

Types of Fish
Primarily brown trout (15 -17") with some rainbows. Also whitefish and golden eye shad.

Known Hatches
Midges, late March - early April through May. Blue winged olives, late April - early June. Pale Morning Duns, mid-July - mid-August, usually midday. Black caddis, mid-August - September, usually p.m.. Tricos late Sept. - Oct.

Equipment to Use
Rods: 9 foot, 4 to 6 weight.
Reels: Click or disc to match rod.
Lines: Weight forward or double taper floating to match rod.
Leaders: 9 foot 4X for nymphing, 5 or 6X for dries.
Wading or Boating: Drift boats get you from hole to hole, but you need to get out and wade the more productive runs. Neoprene waders are best for early spring and fall, while breathables or lightweights are fine for the summer months.

Flies to Use
A "match the hatch" river. Midges #16-20, BWO's #16-18, PMD's #12-18, Black Caddis #16-18, Tricos #18-20. Terrestrials are not used. Fish nymphs midday, dries all day.

When to Fish
April and May, midges as abundant as anglers. If your guide can stay out from 4:30 p.m. to dusk, the fishing is great when midges cluster and most anglers leave. You can see as many as sixty fish feeding at a time. June and July, fewer anglers, more nymphing, but still plenty of dry fly action.

Seasons & Limits
Open year round. Five brown trout, only one can be over 18". Rainbows are strictly catch and release.

Accommodations & Services
Owned and operated by Nick and Francine Forrester, the Big Horn River Resort is high-end at its very best. I recommend their guides Jim McFaydean, Don Lyman, and Fred Charette. An economical alternative is the Big Horn Angler, the oldest fly shop in the area. Clean rooms with private baths. Guide service, as of this writing, runs about $300 a day for boat and two anglers. Ft. Smith has several restaurants and other services.

Rating
Abundant fish and beautiful scenery, a strong 10. To me, Big Horn River Resort is simply heaven on earth.

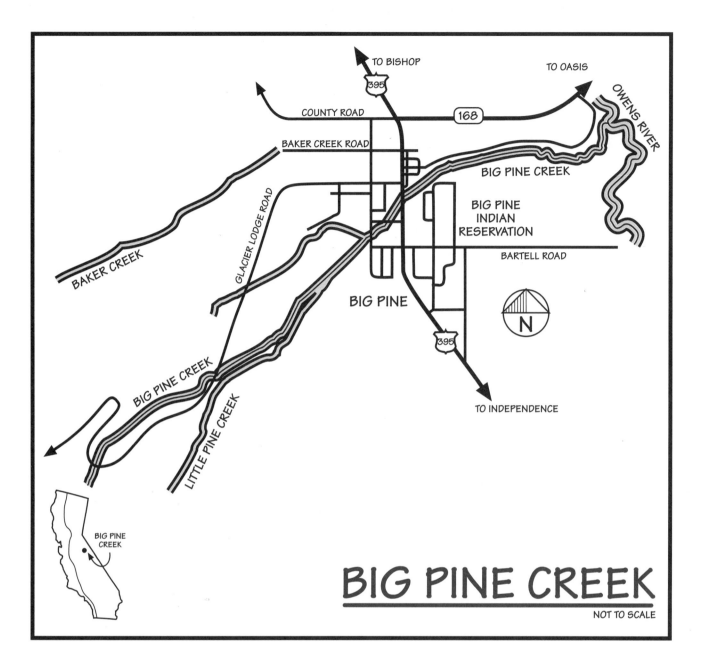

TO BISHOP

TO OASIS

395

OWENS RIVER

COUNTY ROAD

168

BAKER CREEK ROAD

BIG PINE CREEK

BAKER CREEK

GLACIER LODGE ROAD

BIG PINE
INDIAN
RESERVATION

BARTELL ROAD

N

BIG PINE

BIG PINE CREEK

395

LITTLE PINE CREEK

TO INDEPENDENCE

BIG PINE
CREEK

BIG PINE CREEK

NOT TO SCALE

Kate Howe has been an avid angler for over thirty years and is a highly regarded fly tier and instructor. Her fishing travels have taken her to Scotland, England, Japan, and Hawaii as well as from Mexico to Alaska. Working as a licensed guide in Idaho, Nevada, and California completed Kate's fly fishing education. In 1995, she became one of a small group of women in the world ever to land a striped marlin on a fly. Her 112 pounder earned Kate an I.G.F.A. 5 to 1 Club title. She and her husband, Bill, own Classic Anglers, producers of the ALF and FPF, the standard for today's saltwater synthetic flies.

Big Pine Creek
California
Kate Howe

Big fish and big water are not always the key to fly fishing satisfaction. To me, it is the challenge presented by a particular water that makes it great and its ability to make me want to go back for more that makes it special. Big Pine Creek in California's Eastern Sierras is just such a place.

Big Pine Creek's glacial-fed waters wind their way from lakes at the foot of Palisade Glacier, the southern-most ice mass in the U.S., for over fifteen miles to its confluence with the Owens River. The creek's upper reaches are full of ice age cobblestone with waters of a glacial blue-green tint. Traveling down the mountain, Big Pine's cobblestones are replaced by small freestone rocks and sand. By the time it reaches the valley floor, the creek has become a high desert meadow stream with undercut banks and a sandy and rock bottom.

The brown trout of Big Pine Creek are wild and live up to that reputation. Most average around twelve inches with many eight to ten inchers, but the occasional surprise of a sixteen-inch or better brown is a daily event. The creek also has stocked rainbows that add to the mix.

Dry fly fishing on Big Pine Creek can be non-stop in summer after the water temperature has risen and after spring runoff and the hatches stabilize. Nymphing always produces trout and, depending on water depth and cover, usually the bigger fish of the day. Streamer fishing, as well, can be fantastic, giving the angler an opportunity to probe deep pools and undercuts for dominant fish in prime holding water.

Navigating the creek can be tough with lots of brush to negotiate and rocks to climb. It is these areas, however, that produce the best action since many other anglers will not take the time to investigate them. For the faint of heart or leg, there are also easily accessible areas of the creek that are only a short hike from the parking areas.

Big Pine is six hours north of Los Angeles on Highway 395. The fishing starts right in town with more access on Glacier Lodge Road (going west). The eastern section of the creek can be reached by a dirt road off of Highway 168.

Types of Fish
Wild brown trout and stocked rainbows.

Known Hatches & Baitfish
The standard Sierra smorgasbord of caddis, mayflies, stoneflies, terrestrials and trout parr.

Equipment to Use
Rods: 7 to 9 feet, 2 to 5 weight.
Reels: Click or disk to match the rod.
Lines: Weight forward or double taper floating lines.
Leaders: 10' tapered to 5X or 6X.
Wading: Wet wade in the summer. Wear long pants to protect your legs from the brush. In cold weather, hip boots or chest waders. Cleated, felt-soled boots suggested.

Flies to Use
Dries: #14-22, Elk Hair Caddis, Palisade Specials, P.M.D.s.
Nymphs: Gold Ribbed Hare's Ears, Pheasant Tails, caddis pupae are all the nymph fisher needs.
Streamers: Midnight Special, Woolly Bugger, leeches #8-10.

When to Fish
Good all day and into the evening.

Season & Limits
The general trout season opens on the last Saturday in April and closes October 31st. Check current California regulations booklet.

Accommodations & Services
Big Pine has lodging, gas, and groceries as well as two campgrounds. Fly shop in Lee Vining, Mariposa, Bridgeport, Yosemite and Mammoth Lakes (see appendix).

Nearby Fly Fishing
Baker Creek offers another quality small water experience. For bigger water, try the Owens River for browns, rainbows, and bass.

Rating
For the small stream angler, Big Pine Creek rates an 8.

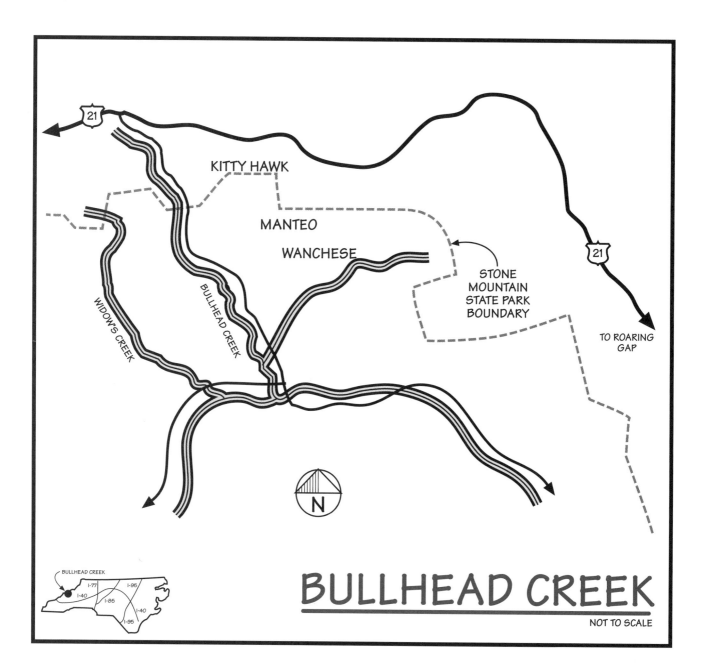

KITTY HAWK

MANTEO

WANCHESE

WIDOW'S CREEK

BULLHEAD CREEK

STONE
MOUNTAIN
STATE PARK
BOUNDARY

TO ROARING
GAP

N

BULLHEAD CREEK

NOT TO SCALE

BULLHEAD CREEK
I-77
I-95
I-40
I-85
I-40
I-95

Rachel Connery has been fishing all her life with her brothers and friends but only for the last five years with a fly rod. In that short time, however, her love of the sport has taken her from Florida to New Hampshire and all over the western U.S.. As a member of the Arizona Women's Fly Fishing Club, Rachel taught fly fishing for the Becoming an Outdoor Woman program and instructed children in fly tying and casting. An FFF Certified Casting Instructor, Rachel is now the director of Mel Krieger's International School of Fly Fishing FISHCAMP, a children's fly fishing summer camp. She lives in Redding, California and works for The Fly Shop.

Bullhead Creek
North Carolina
Rachel Connery

North Carolina's Stone Mountain State Park draws many outdoor enthusiasts. Rock climbers test themselves on the sheer face of a six hundred-foot granite dome. Hikers explore the park's many trails. Anglers wet a line in the magical waters of this mountain paradise.

There are more than a few streams in Stone Mountain State Park where you can fish year round, but the most productive by far is Bull Head Creek. In the heart of the Blue Ridge Mountains, a variety of feeder creeks and springs combine to form this beautiful, small stream.

Bull Head Creek is a catch and release fishery filled with well-educated trout. The fee to fish here is relatively high ($12), but the rewards are great. I've seen trophy sized trout come out of this water. Designated "fly fishing only with net required", this fishery can be very challenging even to the experienced angler.

There are eight sections on the four miles of the Bull Head Creek. Consult an area map for more details on these areas. For the fly angler, sections seven and eight are the largest. Wary and selective browns, rainbows, and brookies fill these sections' deep holes and pools. In these pools, try an indicator, lots of lead and a #14-16 caddis larva. Blue winged olive patterns (dry and nymph) work well on cool, overcast days. In warmer months, cast your high-floating caddis or mayfly dry (with a bead-headed caddis, larva dropper) up into likely looking seams and edges.

Bull Head Creek, in Stone Mountain State Park, is located near the town of Elkin which is only an hour and forty-five minutes from Charlotte, North Carolina. The park is seven miles southwest of Roaring Gap and twenty-five miles northeast of North Wilkesboro.

A dear friend introduced this pristine fishery to me while I was in college. Now that I've shared it with you, please preserve this jewel of a stream and please promote more catch and release on waters across the country.

Types of Fish
Rainbows, browns, and brookies, some native to this stream.

Know Hatches
Caddis, mayflies, stoneflies and midges. In summer, beetles, hoppers and ants.

Equipment to Use
Rods: 7 - 8 foot for small streams, 3 or 4 weight.
Reels: Lightweight, to balance rod.
Lines: Weight forward or double taper floating to match rod.
Leaders: 9 foot or more with 4X, - 6X tippet.
Wading: I prefer waders but wet wading works. Watch those slippery rocks while climbing down to the stream.

Flies to Use
Dries: Light Cahills #16-20, Parachute Adams #14-18, brown, olive, and black Elk Hair Caddis #14-16, Thunderheads #14, sulphurs #16-18.
Nymphs: Pheasant Tails #16-20 (beaded and regular), diving green caddis larvae, beadhead bright green caddis larvae #14-16, soft hackle caddis, mayflies.
Terrestrials: Parachute ants, Dave's Hoppers #14, beetles.

When to Fish
I prefer fall, but spring can also be good. Contact Jesse Brown's Outdoors at 704-556-0020 for a current report.

Seasons & Limits
Fish Bull Head creek year round, fly fishing only, catch and release. Other waters in the park are the same from October 1st until the first Friday in June when they revert to general regulations: 7 fish, any bait or lure.

Accommodations & Services
Stone Mountain State Park, 3042 Frank Parkway, Roaring Gap, NC 28668. Tent sites, grills and tables. At Stone Mountain Cafe, a few miles from the park, get North Carolina BBQ and homemade buttermilk pie. Also, small grocery and restroom. A gas station, before the park entrance, offers homemade chicken salad to go. It's the best!

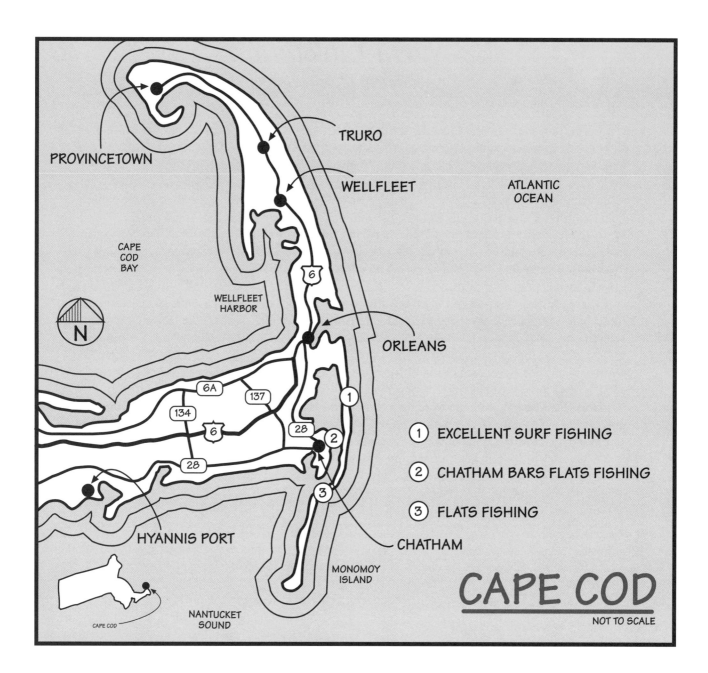

PROVINCETOWN

TRURO

WELLFLEET

ATLANTIC OCEAN

CAPE COD BAY

WELLFLEET HARBOR

N

6

ORLEANS

6A

137

134

6

28

1

28

2

3

① EXCELLENT SURF FISHING

② CHATHAM BARS FLATS FISHING

③ FLATS FISHING

HYANNIS PORT

CHATHAM

MONOMOY ISLAND

CAPE COD

NOT TO SCALE

CAPE COD

NANTUCKET SOUND

Margot Page is the granddaughter of the legendary angling author Sparse Grey Hackle. She is the author of Little Rivers: Tales of a Woman Angler *and serves on the board for Casting for Recovery. The former editor of* The American Fly Fisher, *her articles on fly fishing, the outdoors, and other subjects have appeared in the* New York Times *as well as in* American Health, Countryside, New Woman, Fly Rod & Reel, *and* Trout. *Margot has an M.A. in English literature, briefly taught college English, and worked for fifteen years in magazine and book publishing before becoming a full-time free-lance writer. Her newest book,* Just Horses, *was published in September of 1998.*

Cape Cod Seashore
Massachusetts
Margot Page

*I*n 1961, President Kennedy designated forty miles of coastline along the upper arm of New England's Cape Cod as a National Seashore to be protected forever from development. It's a good thing, because this spectacular stretch of white sand beach and dunes, though eroding five acres a year, still provides the public some of the most spectacular beaches on the East Coast, complete with lighthouses and magnificent surf instead of condos and golf courses.

During the summer season, the beautiful white sand beaches and sand flats around Chatham draw throngs of people, but these beaches are also a favorite mecca of the glorious striped bass and other species. Pods of thousands of fish range up and down the arm of the Cape, and, if you're favored by Lady Luck, you'll stumble upon a slashing blitz of churning water, flipping baitfish, and tons of gulls.

If you're not acquainted with the area, your best bet is to contact local sporting dealers or shops to find one of the excellent guides in the area. One of their favorite methods to fish the area is to take you in a four-wheeler on dune roads to a remote location on the beach where you can surfcast. Cape Cod guides will also use flats boats to fish the spectacular flats around Monomoy Point as well as to fish offshore. This is my favorite kind of fishing: soft white sand, ocean, wild and wooly action, and big beautiful fish.

Types of Fish
Offshore: Striped bass, bonito, false albacore, blue fish, and flounder.
Shore: Striped bass, blue fish, flounder, and, infrequently, bonito and false albacore.

Equipment to Use
Rods: 9 foot, 7 to 10 weight.
Reels: Any durable saltwater reel with appropriate line. 150 yards of backing is sufficient.
Lines: Weight forward floating, Clear Tip, Depth Charge, and shooting heads.
Leaders: 9 foot, 12 to 16 pound for everything except blues which need a wire shock tippet.
Wading: Chest high breathable or neoprene waders and boots.
Other: Polarized glasses, stripping basket, rain jacket, sun protection.

Flies to Use
Chernobyl Crabs, Flexo-Crabs, Epoxy Sand Eels #4 - 8, Gurglers #1/0, Deceivers and Clousers #6, 4, 2, 2/0 in olive/white, yellow/white, and chartreuse.

When to Fish
May - October for striped bass and bluefish.
August - September for bonito.
August - October for false albacore.
Year round for flounder.

Accommodations & Services
For accommodations in the coastal towns of Chatham, Orleans, Eastham, Truro, Wellfleet, and Provincetown call 1-888-33CAPECOD.
On the internet: www.CapeCodChamber.org.
Area tackle dealers and shops can help you find local guides (see appendix).

Rating
One of nature's classically beautiful coastlines combined with hot fishing . . . hmmm, whaddaya think?

Editors Note: Sounds like a 10 to us!

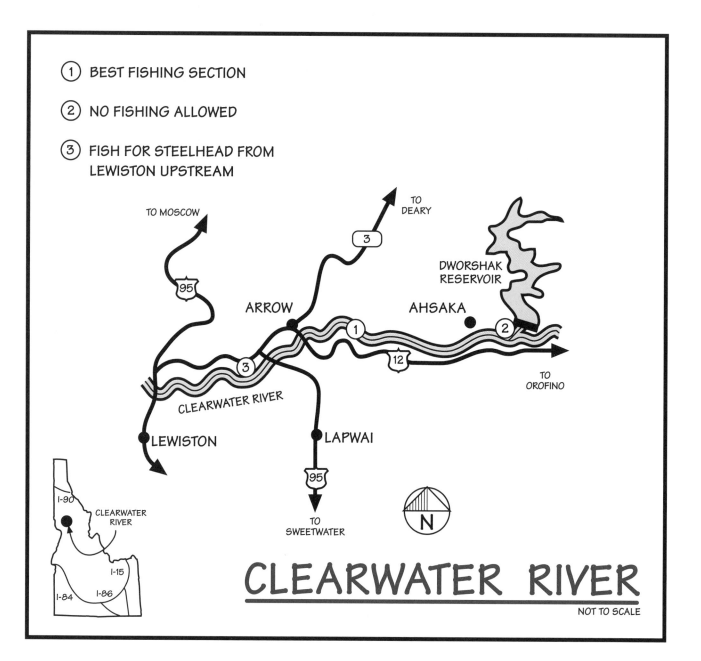

1 BEST FISHING SECTION

2 NO FISHING ALLOWED

3 FISH FOR STEELHEAD FROM
LEWISTON UPSTREAM

TO MOSCOW

TO DEARY

3

DWORSHAK
RESERVOIR

95

ARROW

AHSAKA

1

2

12

TO OROFINO

CLEARWATER RIVER

3

LEWISTON

LAPWAI

95

TO SWEETWATER

N

I-90

CLEARWATER RIVER

I-15

I-84   I-86

CLEARWATER RIVER

NOT TO SCALE

Janet Downey's two-year courtship consisted of future husband Marty teaching her how to cast a fly rod. In 1981, the pair married aboard a drift boat on the Boise River and went on a steelhead fishing honeymoon. In 1983, Janet started Angler's Expressions which designs and manufactures fishing related gift items. Angler's Expressions employs twenty people and supplies thousands of accounts worldwide. With both of their vocations rooted in the fly fishing industry, Janet and Marty, a manufacturer's representative for Cortland Line Company, have been able to travel and fish together throughout the world.

Clearwater River
Idaho
Janet Downey

*T*he Clearwater River in northern Idaho is one of the few steelhead rivers in the lower forty-eight states where it's still possible to catch a 12-15 pound summer steelhead. Here you can experience the excitement and anticipation of catching these wild fish on a fly rod, but be fore-warned … angling for these Idaho "gems" may prove to be a humbling test of your fly fishing skills.

For Pacific steelhead compelled by genetic instinct to return to their spawning grounds, the Clearwater River is the end of a seven hundred mile journey up the Columbia and Snake Rivers. Named because of its crystalline waters, the Clearwater's extremely rocky bottom creates perfect resting places for travel-weary steelhead and the occasional salmon. As of this writing, Clearwater steelhead are listed as "threatened" under the Endangered Species Act. No wild steelhead (defined as any rainbow trout over 20") may be kept at any time.

Clearwater steelhead can be caught with dry and wet flies, depending on the sun, the clouds, or the barometer. However, the most exciting way to catch these fish is using a floating line and a sparsely tied fly designed either to ride high in the water column or to skitter right on top, waking across the current. No one knows why, but steelhead love to come up and take a fly near or on the surface. Most times you can see a bulge of water or even the fish's head as it comes up to take the fly. Now, you must keep the rod still and wait for the line to come tight as the fish turns away. Be prepared when she feels the sting of the hook. Typically steelhead runs are strong and acrobatic; keep the line tight and follow the fish. If you land her, your time and effort will be well rewarded. You'll have to earn this thrill, so dress warm and have patience. It will be worth the pain!

Between Lewiston and Orofino, Idaho, forty miles of Highway 12 parallels the Clearwater and provides numerous pullouts. Spots such as the Stink Hole (by the paper pulp factory), Coyote, Fish Net, Junkyard Hole, Haystack, and Cherry Lane Bridge hold fish, but you have to get up very early to put the first fly through these well-known fishing holes.

Types of Fish
Steelhead, chinook salmon, rainbow and cutthroat trout.

Known Hatches
Steelhead are not feeding. Flies are an irritant or attractor.

Equipment to Use
Rods: 9 to 14 foot, 8 or 9 weight, single or double handed.
Reels: Single action, smooth drag with 150 yards of backing.
Lines: Weight forward floating to cover the water. If unsuccessful, try a shooting head or sink-tip.
Leaders: 9 or 10 foot, 10 to 15 pound tippet.
Wading: River depth, because of clarity, is very deceiving; be careful! Wear neoprene waders, a belt and use a staff.

Flies to Use
Various colors of traditional steelhead flies with two-tone bodies and hairwings. With sinking lines, buggy nymphs, skating dry flies, big marabou streamers, or Woolly Buggers with prominent silhouettes.

When to Fish
Mid-October to April for steelhead that stay over the winter and spawn in the spring. July to September, catch & release: fewer jet boats and summer steelhead fishing is prime.

Seasons & Limits
Open year-round. From May 1st to October 15th no steelhead may be harvested. Fall and spring, two/day, four in possession limit on hatchery fish (identified by their clipped adipose fin). Season limit of ten.

Accommodations & Services
Motels, restaurants and other services in Lewiston and Orofino. Camping in KOA's and other areas.

Nearby Fly Fishing
The Snake River for steelhead. Surrounding mountain lakes and streams for trout.

Rating
The Clearwater is a definite 10!

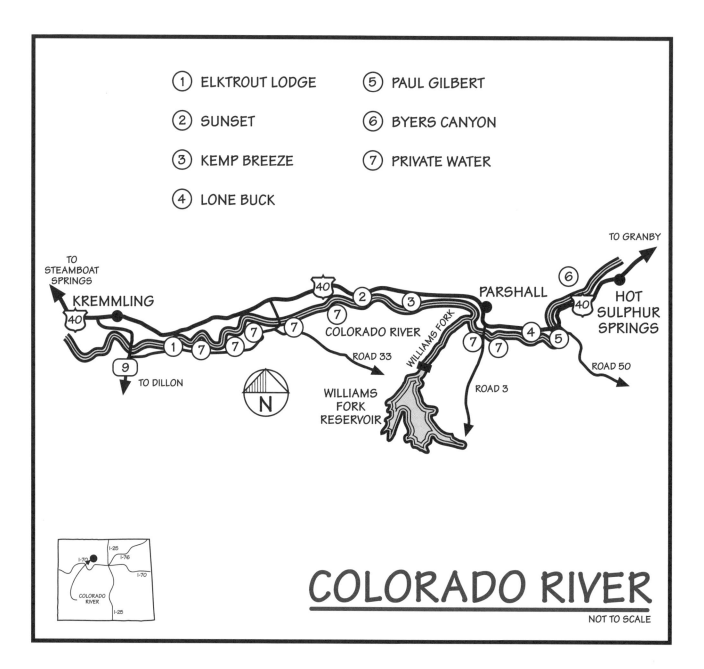

1. ELKTROUT LODGE
2. SUNSET
3. KEMP BREEZE
4. LONE BUCK
5. PAUL GILBERT
6. BYERS CANYON
7. PRIVATE WATER

TO STEAMBOAT SPRINGS

KREMMLING

TO DILLON

40

9

1

7

7

7

7

COLORADO RIVER

ROAD 33

N

WILLIAMS FORK RESERVOIR

WILLIAMS FORK

40

2

3

PARSHALL

ROAD 3

7

7

4

5

6

TO GRANBY

HOT SULPHUR SPRINGS

40

ROAD 50

I-25
I-76
I-70
I-70
COLORADO RIVER
I-25

COLORADO RIVER

NOT TO SCALE

Jean Williams has been a professional guide since 1994. Orvis endorsed, she still teaches at the Rocky Mountain Orvis Schools sponsored by the Blue Quill Angler. Her guiding also includes working with The Master Angler as well as the prestigious Elktrout Lodge. Jean is the founder of Colorado Women Fly Fishers, and she is a member of International Women Fly Fishers, Federation of Fly Fishers, and Trout Unlimited. An avid and generous volunteer for the resource and much sought after as an outdoor speaker, Jean is passionate about fly fishing. She enjoys sharing this passion with various friends and family members, including her brother, Michael, also a fishing and whitewater guide.

Colorado River
Colorado
Jean Williams

Born in the heart of Rocky Mountain National Park, the Colorado River runs through Middle Park between Hot Sulphur Springs and Kremmling, Colorado. With its deep runs, teasing riffles, and glassy flats, this is classic western trout water with some very challenging fly fishing, great scenery and outstanding, big water fishing.

Two hours west of Denver and paralleling US Highway 40, this Gold Medal Water sweeps through the pristine beauty of ancient cottonwood groves, homesteaded ranches, and mountain meadows. The wild trout here are extremely wary. Stay low when approaching and take time to observe. Limit false casts, and dissect the water into likely looking prime channels and lies. Recently the rainbows were decimated by whirling disease. As of this writing they've been re-stocked. Colorado and Snake River, fine-spotted cutthroat trout are also available.

You can dry fly fish the Colorado with everything from a #8 Stimulator down to a #28 trico. As with all dry fly fishing, line control is paramount. Try fishing two flies: a large dry fly as the indicator and a small emerger pattern as the dropper about 22" below the dry. This offers hungry trout two flavors in one pass.

Traditionally, "high sticking" or "short-line nymphing" has proven to be the most effective way to nymph fish the Colorado. Keep your nymph drifting drag-free by holding as much of the fly line off the water as possible. When high sticking, I use a tea or light peach colored strike indicator and enough non-toxic weight to get my fly down on the bottom. Long-line nymphing is another excellent technique which allows a more stealthy presentation, faster fly sink rate, and a tighter line than short-lining. And don't be afraid to use the two-fly system with nymphs.

The Colorado River offers easy access, exceptional beauty, and challenging fly fishing. With outstanding dry fly, nymph, and streamer fishing, this river provides an excellent opportunity for a "technical grand slam."

Types of Fish
Brown, rainbow and cutthroat trout and brookies.

Known Hatches
Spring: Stoneflies, caddis, pale evening duns.
Early Summer: BWO's, red quills, small green drakes, PMD's.
Late Summer: Tricos, western olives, damsels, ants, hoppers.
Fall: Beetles, BWO's, midges, leeches, forage fish.

Equipment to Use
Rods: 7 to 9 foot, 4 or 5 weight. Stiff action for casting in the frequent late afternoon wind.
Reels: Disk drag.
Lines: Weight forward or double tapered floating. Sink-tip for deeper water nymphing and streamer fishing.
Leaders: Generally 9 to 12' tapered to 4, 5, or 6X.
Wading: Deep runs, fast riffles, use chest waders with belt and sturdy, felt-soled boots. Late summer river bottom algae is slippery, wade with care.

Flies to Use
Dries: Yellow Sally, Trude, BWO, Z-Lon Baetis, Adams, Wulff, PMD, rusty spinners, Red Quill, Elk Hair Caddis, Trico, Griffith's Gnat, Hoppers, Para-Ants, Mouse.
Nymphs: Stones, Halfback, Bitch Creek, 20-Incher, Hare's Ear, Breadcrust, caddis, Prince, RS2, Brassie, Pheasant Tail, Buckskin, Miracle, Black Beauty, Loop Wing, Midge Biot.
Streamers: Wooly Bugger, Grey Ghost, Matuka, Cone-Head Muddler, Zonker, Leech.

When to Fish
All year.

Season & Limits
Year-round fishing, artificial flies and lures only. Return all trout to the water immediately.

Accommodations & Services
All services in Hot Sulphur Springs, Parshall, and Kremmling. See Appendix.

Nearby Fly Fishing
Williams' Fork Reservoir, Blue and Eagle Rivers.

Rating
I give it a 7 to 10 depending on when you fish it.

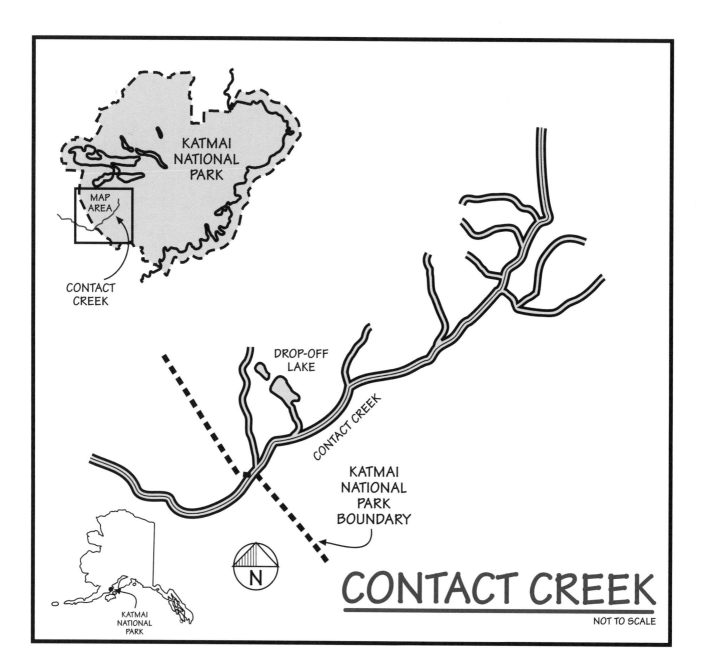

KATMAI
NATIONAL
PARK

MAP
AREA

CONTACT
CREEK

DROP-OFF
LAKE

CONTACT CREEK

KATMAI
NATIONAL
PARK
BOUNDARY

N

KATMAI
NATIONAL
PARK

CONTACT CREEK

NOT TO SCALE

Nanci Morris owns and operates Katmai Fishing Adventures. She has been using her captain's and pilot's licenses to help anglers experience the thrill of fly fishing for Bristol Bay's trophy rainbow and salmon for over fourteen years. During Alaska's "off season," Nanci can be found fishing warm waters around the world where she has landed most species of saltwater fish and set several world records, including one for striped marlin. She has appeared on several national television shows about fresh and saltwater fly fishing and is also an instructor for the Bonefish School at the Peace and Plenty Lodge in the Bahamas.

Contact Creek
Alaska
Nanci Morris

*I*f your definition of "quality fishing" includes variety of fish, remoteness, spectacular beauty, and wildlife, you could not choose a more perfect destination than Alaska's Contact Creek. This unique fishery offers a rare opportunity to sample all of the above and more in a single trip.

Contact Creek is located a short, thirty-five minute floatplane trip west of King Salmon in the heart of Katmai National Park. Nestled in the Alaska Range, this clear water stream originates in Yori Pass and ends at the King Salmon River. The creek is fishable after the initial spring run off from mid-June through August.

Lined by alder, ash and spruce, Contact Creeks sparkling waters hold native rainbow trout, arctic char, and grayling throughout its short, fishable season, as well as sockeye, chum and king salmon (summer). Sightings of brown bear, moose, eagle, fox, tundra swan, wolverine, wolves, caribou, and an endless variety of waterfowl are not uncommon, even if your stay is limited to one day. One can be moved from a piece of water by brown bear that decide to claim your fishing run.

During late June and July, dry flies and mouse patterns are highly effective for all of the native species. If salmon are your goal, this wadeable water offers an excellent opportunity to sight cast to large fish using weighted streamers and dry lines. Even the mighty and elusive king salmon becomes catchable in this small stream.

The trip to Contact Creek requires a degree of physical fitness. A float plane drops you off at a lake approximately a mile from the creek. The hike is an enjoyable experience in and of itself if you take your time and enjoy the scenery. Late in the season, sample the low bush cranberries, blueberries, salmonberries, and crowberries that line the trail to the creek. Often bears are grazing on the slopes near the trail while moose and caribou wander across open stretches.

Types of Fish
June - August, rainbow trout, arctic char, grayling. July - August, sockeye, chum, king salmon.

Known Hatches
Periodic stonefly, caddis and mayfly hatches.

Equipment to Use
Rods: 7 to 8 foot, 4 to 6 weight rods for small species. 7 to 9 weight for salmon.
Reels: Click fine for small fish. Big disc drag for salmon!
Lines: Weight forward or double taper floating to match rod.
Leaders: 7 to 9 foot, 6 lb., with or without strike indicator, for small species. 6 to 8 foot, 10 - 20 lb. for salmon.
Wading: Using care and caution, you can wade most of the creek. Use a staff for confidence.

Flies to Use
Dries: Humpy, Royal Wulff, Coachman, mosquito, Adams #12-14. Mice, vole for rainbows beneath undercut banks.
Nymphs: Pheasant Tail, Hare's Ear, Prince #10-14.
Streamers: Wooly Bugger, leech, muddler, sculpin. Roe and flesh #2-6. Flashy bugger, streamer for salmon #1/0-2.

When to Fish
Native species late June - July. Salmon run mid-July until late August.

Seasons & Limits
Open June - April, but inaccessible much of that time. Keeping fish not recommended due to danger posed by bear.

Accommodations & Services
King Salmon, with a year round population of 450 (swells during the fishing season) has three restaurants and bars, general store and liquor store. Several float plane businesses operate along the Naknek River near town.

Nearby Fly Fishing
Try the Naknek River, a trophy fishery. Numerous tributaries and additional fly-out destinations readily available.

Rating
Depending on your view of accessibility the rating is a 9. I find the remoteness an asset and rank Contact Creek a 10 on my list of Bristol Bay's available fishing water.

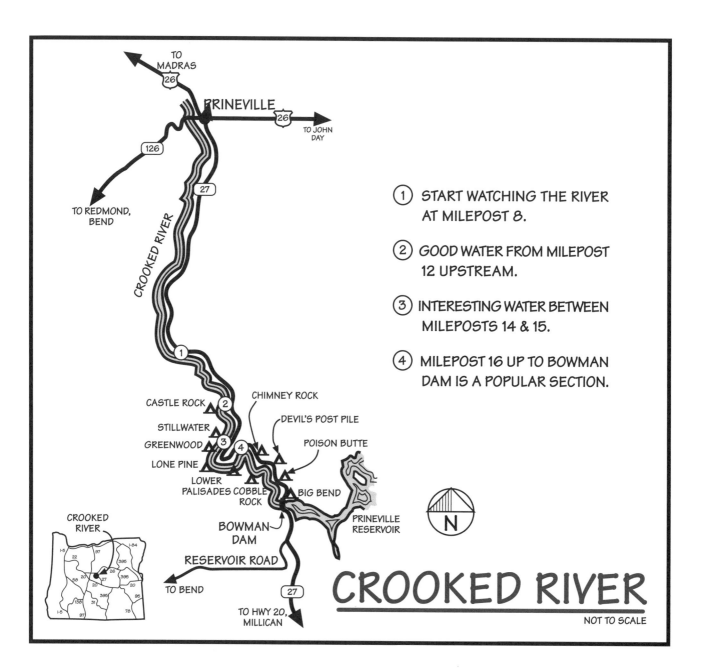

TO MADRAS
26

PRINEVILLE
26
TO JOHN DAY

126

27

TO REDMOND, BEND

CROOKED RIVER

1

① START WATCHING THE RIVER AT MILEPOST 8.

② GOOD WATER FROM MILEPOST 12 UPSTREAM.

③ INTERESTING WATER BETWEEN MILEPOSTS 14 & 15.

④ MILEPOST 16 UP TO BOWMAN DAM IS A POPULAR SECTION.

CASTLE ROCK
2
CHIMNEY ROCK
STILLWATER
GREENWOOD
3
4
DEVIL'S POST PILE
LONE PINE
POISON BUTTE
LOWER PALISADES COBBLE ROCK
BIG BEND
BOWMAN DAM
PRINEVILLE RESERVOIR
RESERVOIR ROAD

N

CROOKED RIVER

CROOKED RIVER

TO BEND

27

TO HWY 20, MILLICAN

CROOKED RIVER

NOT TO SCALE

Madelynne "Maddy" Sheehan is a "fishing buddy" to thousands of anglers through her award-winning guide book, Fishing in Oregon. *The ninth edition, published by Maddy's company, Flying Pencil Publications, was recently released. Maddy is one of the few women publishers of fishing books with titles such as* Fishing in Oregon's Deschutes River *and* Fishing in Oregon's Best Fly Waters. *Maddy lives in Scappoose, Oregon where, these days, she devotes more of her time to fish restoration than to fishing. She is a founding member of the Scappoose Bay Watershed Council. Maddy also won the ISE "Best of the West" Women's Fly Casting Championship in Portland.*

Crooked River
Oregon
Maddy Sheehan

*I*f you love the subtle beauty of desert canyons, the scent of sage, and lots of solitude, consider the "off-season" of central Oregon's Crooked River. From fall to spring, when other streams are swollen and their trout scattered, this high desert river's rainbows are at their best.

The most productive and accessible stretch of the Crooked River is the seven miles below Bowman Dam. This is a classic tailrace fishery. The naturally rich alkaline flow is enhanced by moderated releases of cold water from the bottom of Prineville Reservoir. While not known for large trout, there is both quantity and quality—in some years, over 6,000 plump, native rainbows per river mile. The average catch is 8-12". There is always the possibility of a 2-3 lb., nineteen-incher. Releasing fish over 13" is encouraged.

Crooked River trout are accustomed to turbid conditions year round and are most relaxed when the river is running full. There are plenty of fish within 15' of the east bank trail. During low flows, by wading carefully, you can often fish over to the west bank.

Don't be put off by the brown cast of the water. Trout see your #18 fly even if you can't! Look for subtle sipping rather than flashy rises. Mayfly hatch or not, try small brown or olive nymph imitations. There are occasional caddis hatches in spring and fall. Weighted orange scud imitations and midge pupae can also be very effective.

Nine BLM campgrounds and three picnic areas with interconnecting trails offer pleasant though primitive facilities and excellent river access. The campsites are small and cost $5/day. Only Chimney Rock Campground has drinking water. The most coveted campgrounds are closest to the dam, but with the concentration of fish, you can often catch dozens of trout per day from any camp.

If you're driving to the Crooked River from the east in mid-autumn, treat yourself to the Highway 26 route through the Blue and Ochoco Mountains with their golden tamaracks and crimson patches of roadside huckleberries. To reach the river from Prineville on Highway 26, follow the signs to Bowman Dam, turning south onto Highway 27. Don't follow signs to Prineville Reservoir. Highway 27 hugs the east bank of the river all the way to the dam.

Types of Fish
Native redband rainbows and large whitefish.

Known Hatches
Blue winged olives, caddis, midges, and scuds.

Equipment to Use
Rods: 6 to 9 foot, 3-5 weight.
Reels: Click or disc to match rod.
Lines: Weight forward or double taper floating.
Leaders: 9 foot tapered to 4 lbs. Fine leaders rarely needed.
Wading: Waders or hip boots. Easy walking.

Flies to Use
Dries: Mayfly (olive body with white or gray wing) #10-18, tan body caddis #16.
Nymphs: Pheasant Tail or Hare's Ear (olive, gray, tan), beadhead scuds (olive-gray, tan, orange) #10-18, midge pupae #18-24. Egg pattern in December when whitefish spawn.

When to Fish
Mid-September to mid-May, mid-morning to dark. No need to get up early to fish here.

Seasons & Limits
Catch & release only for trout November 1st - April 23rd. Five fish per day at other times. No limit on whitefish.

Accommodations & Services
Prineville, 12 miles away, has motels, restaurants, general services, and a fly shop. An easy day outing from Bend or Sisters where there are extensive facilities and services.

Nearby Fly Fishing
The Deschutes, Metolius and Fall rivers.

Rating
Most years an 8 for fish quantity and size. For beauty, accessibility, and solitude on an autumn afternoon, a 9.

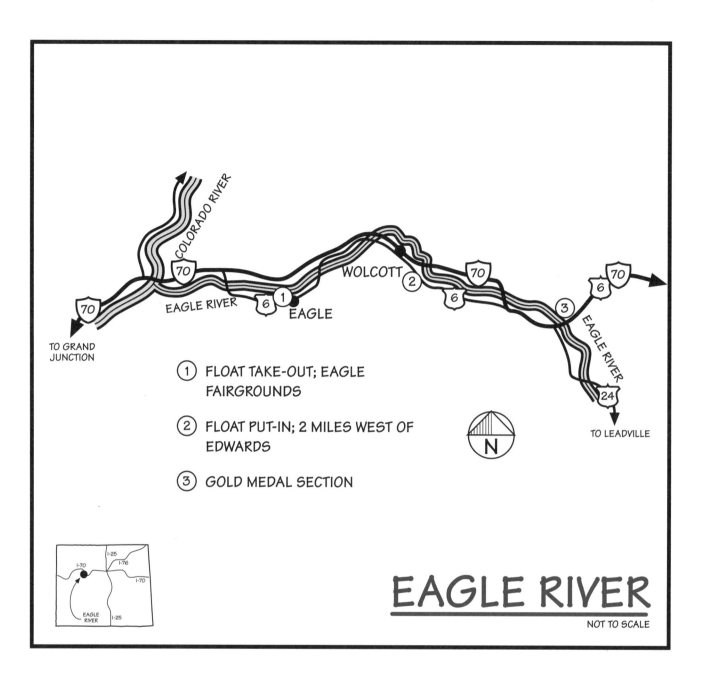

① FLOAT TAKE-OUT; EAGLE
   FAIRGROUNDS

② FLOAT PUT-IN; 2 MILES WEST OF
   EDWARDS

③ GOLD MEDAL SECTION

EAGLE RIVER

NOT TO SCALE

Cindy Scholl has been guiding in Colorado's Vail Valley for 7 years. She is currently the only female guide that oars a boat. Her enthusiasm, knowledge and professionalism make her one of the most respected and sought after guides in the area. She is an active participant and Secretary for the local Trout Unlimited Chapter. She also gives presentations on entomology and fishing techniques. She served on the Women and Guiding panel and festival committee for the International Women's Fly Fishing Festival. She currently serves as an IWFF board member. Cindy is also a certified shooting instructor and field trial judge and is an experienced shooter, dog handler and trainer.

Eagle River
Colorado
Cynthia Scholl

Described as one of the world's premiere resort areas, the Eagle Valley attracts tourists, sports enthusiasts and fly fishermen alike. From its headwaters high in the Sawatch Range to its confluence with the Colorado River, the Eagle River stretches seventy miles through alpine forests down to the valley floor. Whether you're an expert looking to improve your technical fly fishing skills or a novice in need of an excellent learning environment, the Eagle River is the place to visit.

The character of the Eagle River with its endless pocket water, riffles, bends, and pools can best be described as diverse, and, happily, it is fishable most of the year. During late winter and early spring, nymph fishing is the most productive technique. Look for deep pools where the trout have congregated due to the low water level. Snow melt and heavy run-off make for perilous fishing in May and June.

After run-off, Eagle River trout move into "feeding stations" behind boulders and submerged rocks. Wade carefully into these areas; the bottom can be very slippery! Abundant vegetation along the river's edge provides superb cover for the prolific caddis hatches of June and July, a great time to tie on a dry attractor with a caddis pupa dropper. Late summer brings excellent terrestrial fishing. Trail an ant behind your hopper, and you're bound to land a feisty trout. These trout are not highly selective, so "matching the hatch" is not as important as the presentation of your fly.

Floating the Eagle is an excellent way to fish more water or water that is not accessible by wading, but the "float season" only lasts a few short summer months due to fluctuating water levels. Your best bet is to hire a local guide. While he or she rows, you can fish and enjoy the beautiful scenery!

The Eagle River has many public access points from Highway 6 just off Interstate 70. To ensure a safe and enjoyable trip, pick up a public access map at any of the local fly shops.

Types of Fish
Brown, rainbow, cutthroat trout, and brookies.

Known Hatches
Midges, stoneflies, caddis, mayflies (Baetis, PMD's, green drakes, red quills) and terrestrials.

Equipment to Use
Rods: 8 to 9 foot, 4 - 6 weight.
Reels: Click or disc drag to match rod.
Lines: Weight forward or double taper floating.
Leaders: 7 to 9 foot, 4 - 6X.
Wading: Neoprene waders and felt-soled boots.

Flies to Use
Dries: Griffith's Gnat #16-22, Adams #14-20, caddis #12-18, BWO, blue and red quill #16-20, green drake #10-12, PMD, red and black ant, little yellow stone #14-18, golden stone #8-10. Royal Wulff, Royal Humpy, Stimulator #10-16.
Nymphs: Gold Ribbed Hare's Ear, Prince #12-18, Pheasant Tail #14-20, Zug Bug #12-16, caddis larvae and pupae #14-18, Halfback #6-10, golden stone #8-12, RS2 emerger, Brassie #16-20, Disco Midge, all colors #18-22.
Streamers: Wooly Bugger #4-10, Muddler Minnow #4-8.

When to Fish
July - September best time for dry fly fishing. Spring, prior to run-off, nymphing is superb, and the occasional cloudy day can produce excellent Baetis and midge hatches. Late fall, large Stimulators bring fish to the surface.

Season & Limits
Open year-round. Two fish limit with no size restriction.

Accommodations & Services
The town of Eagle has grocery stores, fly shops, motels, and gas. There are two campsites near Gypsum and BLM campsite just west of Wolcott with limited facilities. Cindy Scholl at Gorsuch Outfitters, Vail, 1-877-476-4700 or e-mail, scholls@sni.net.

Nearby Fly Fishing
The Blue, Roaring Fork and Colorado Rivers, Gore Creek.

Rating
Compared to other mountain trout streams, the Eagle is a great producer, a solid 8.

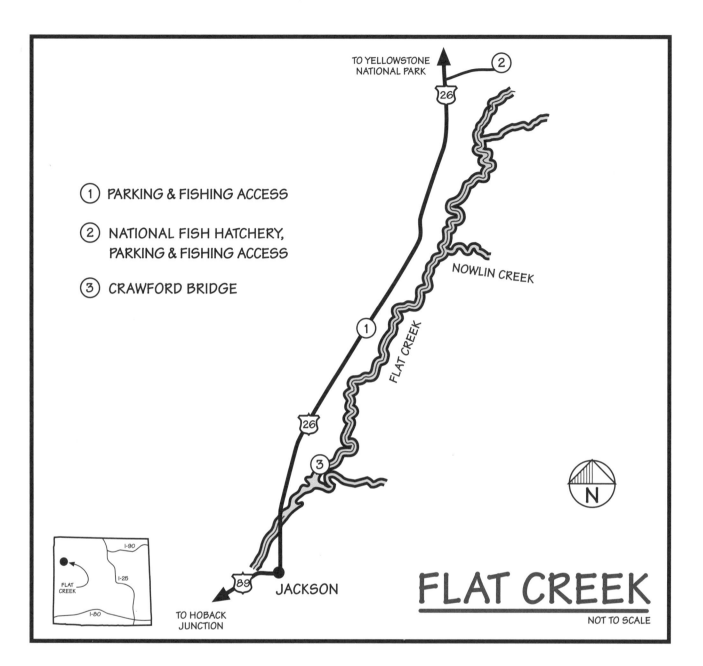

1 PARKING & FISHING ACCESS

2 NATIONAL FISH HATCHERY,
PARKING & FISHING ACCESS

3 CRAWFORD BRIDGE

TO YELLOWSTONE
NATIONAL PARK

26

2

NOWLIN CREEK

FLAT CREEK

1

26

3

N

I-90

I-25

FLAT
CREEK

I-80

89

JACKSON

TO HOBACK
JUNCTION

FLAT CREEK

NOT TO SCALE

Patty Reilly is a familiar face in the fishing community. She is a twenty-year freshwater guide and casting instructor who began her professional fishing career in Wyoming, guiding out of rafts and dories on the Snake River and surrounding waters. Her teaching and guiding have taken her to Colorado, Montana, Idaho, and Alaska. In the late seventies, Patty and a partner began an outfitting company in Argentina, in effect laying the groundwork for the fly fishing guide business in Patagonia. Currently she is the Director of Fishing Operations for the Crescent H Ranch, an Orvis endorsed fishing lodge in Jackson Hole, Wyoming.

Flat Creek
Wyoming
Patty Reilly

*T*he headwaters of Wyoming's Flat Creek originate high in the Gros Ventre mountain range and flow below the Sleeping Indian, the most prominent landmark in Jackson Hole. In the valley, the creek becomes a classic, meandering, meadow stream that is home to a healthy population of indigenous Snake River cutthroat trout. Flat Creek offers easy access, beautiful scenery, and the possibility of catching a large cutthroat, a fun and exciting combination for even the most experienced angler.

Flat Creek winds its way through the heart of the National Elk Refuge, which serves as a winter home to seven-to-nine thousand elk as well as Rocky Mountain bighorn sheep and bison. In the summer, the grassy meadows around the creek are a haven for trumpeter swans and other species of waterfowl, raptor, and songbird. In the 1980's, Trout Unlimited, the U.S. Fish and Wildlife Service, and the Wyoming Department of Fish and Game undertook a habitat restoration project to repair the damage to the creek bed caused by years of grazing elk and sedimentation from spring run-off. Today, ample evidence of the success of the project can be found in the stream's abundant insect life, the good numbers of all ages of trout, and, consequently, the greatly improved fishing.

Patience and care are your best tools for fishing Flat Creek. The creek's banks are undercut, and vibrations from walking too close to the edge may cause you to spook fish. You should keep a low profile and watch for working fish. Matching an existing hatch offers you the best chance of hooking one of the creek's wild cutthroat, but at the right time of the year, a terrestrial, especially a grasshopper pattern, can be equally effective. If you find that the trout are not working, you can always hook a whitefish by nymphing the riffles. Check with local fly shops for the best hatch times as well as patterns that are working.

Because of its easy access, breathtaking surroundings, and wild cutthroat, Flat Creek has to be one of the premier trout streams in the western United States. If you find yourself in the Jackson, Wyoming area, I could not recommend a better place for you to wet a line.

Types of Fish
Native Snake River cutthroat and Rocky Mountain whitefish.

Known Hatches & Baitfish
Tricos, gray drakes, PMD's, caddis, BWO's, grasshopper, and sculpins.

Equipment to Use
Rods: 8 to 9 foot, 4 - 6 weight.
Reels: Click or disc to match rod.
Lines: Double taper or weight forward floating.
Leaders: 9 to 10 foot, 3 - 7X.
Wading: Hippers are fine.

Flies to Use
Dries: Match known hatches or use all purpose flies such as #18 Adams, PMD's, ants.
Nymphs: Pheasant Tail, Hare's Ear, emergers, peeking caddis.
Streamers: Muddler Minnow.

When to Fish
Naturally, the best times are during hatches, but any time of the day can be productive. Check local shops for hatch conditions.

Season & Limits
Flat Creek has limited fishing boundaries and seasonal access due to nesting waterfowl, so be sure to check Wyoming fishing regulations.

Accommodations & Services
A wide variety available. Jackson Chamber of Commerce, (307) 733-3316 for motels, hotels.

Nearby Fly Fishing
The Snake, South Fork of the Snake, and Green rivers.

Rating
Flat Creek can be a 10, depending on the cooperation of the fish and the skill level of the angler.

TO
BOZEMAN

SWAN
CREEK

MOOSE
CREEK

191

GALLATIN RIVER

PORTAL
CREEK

TO BIG
SKY
RESORT

① GALLATIN RIVERGUIDES

② GOOD BOULDERS

③ RIFFLES

④ RED CLIFF

PORCUPINE CREEK

③

GALLATIN RIVER

④

BUFFALO
HORN CREEK

191

②

N

TAYLOR
FORK
ROAD

I-90 I-15 I-94

I-15 I-90

GALLATIN
RIVER

TO WEST
YELLOWSTONE

GALLATIN RIVER

NOT TO SCALE

Betsey French moved to Montana in 1980. She and her husband, Steve, have owned and operated Gallatin Riverguides, a fly fishing outfitting and retail store on the Gallatin River in Big Sky for over sixteen years. Betsey has been teaching women fly fishing courses in the area for the last five years and enthusiastically urges more women to take up the sport. Currently Betsey is vice president of International Women Fly Fishers. She and Steve are the proud parents of two freckle-faced, red-haired girls, Kelsey and Bridget.

Gallatin River
Montana
Betsey French

Named for Secretary of the Treasury, Albert Gallatin, by Lewis & Clark, the Gallatin River is considered a masterpiece freestone river. From its headwaters in the northwest corner of Yellowstone National Park, the river flows north through the heart of the Gallatin Canyon where, at Three Forks, it joins the Madison and Jefferson Rivers to form the Missouri. This jewel of a stream boasts rainbows, browns, and hybrid cuttbows that challenge the most experienced angler.

Because of the variety of accessible water, my favorite section of the Gallatin River runs through the Gallatin Canyon near the resort of Big Sky. You can travel 10 miles north or south of the resort and find a wealth of gentle riffles, boulder-strewn pocket water, meadow runs, tree-lined cut-banks, and fast moving white water. Bring a camera, for the abundant wildlife, vibrant wildflowers, and blue skies are memories you'll want to take home.

Each year after the spring run off, usually around the end of June, the banks of the Gallatin come alive with insects. Like many western streams, this is primarily a caddis river, but I always look forward to the stonefly/salmon fly hatch. Casting large Sofa Pillows, Bird Stones, and rusty Stimulators to aggressive trout make for an exciting afternoon. As mentioned, a good variety of caddis are abundant as well as mayflies, so keep plenty of those patterns in your vest as well. The Gallatin is also wonderful nymph water. Throughout the summer, use Prince Nymphs, Hare's Ears, and Peeking Caddis.

From mid-July to August, terrestrials make their appearance. Fish meadow sections and grassy banks using your favorite hopper, ant, or beetle. In autumn, stripping Wooly Buggers, Zonkers, and Matukas in front of aggressive pre-spawn brown trout will almost certainly net you a nice fish.

Finally, when you visit the Gallatin, please practice "CPR," catch, photograph, and release, for the protection and future of this terrific fishery. After you discover the wonderful secret of this river, why don't we just keep it between the two of us.

Types of Fish
Rainbows, browns, and hybrid cuttbows.

Known Hatches
Stone & salmon flies, caddis, mayflies, midges, terrestrials.

Equipment to Use
Rods: 8 to 9 foot, 3 - 5 weight.
Reels: Click or disc drag to match rod.
Lines: Weight forward or double taper floating.
Leaders: 7 to 9 foot, 4 to 6X.
Wading: Slippery rocks in gin-clear water. Waders, felt-soled shoes, wading staff. July - August, wet wade. Polarized sunglasses a must.

Flies to Use
Dries: Sofa Pillow #2-4, Bird's Stone #2-6 (June-July), Rusty Stimulator, golden stone #4-10 (July-Aug). Elk Hair Caddis (July-Sept.), X-Caddis #12-18 (July-Aug). PMD #14-18, speckled dun, Callibaetis #12-14, trico #20-24 (July-Aug), Parachute Adams #14-18 (May-Sept). Midge, Griffith's Gnat #18-22 (Winter/Spring). Hopper #8-14, flying ant #14-28, black beetle #14-18 (July-Sept). Trude, Humpy, Wulff, Stimu-lator, H & L Variant (July-Sept).
Nymphs: Prince, Hare's Ear, Pheasant Tail, Serendipitie #12-16, Swallow #8-12, Amber Stone #10-15 (all year).
Streamers: Wooly Bugger, Zonker, and Matuka, #2-8.

When to Fish
Summer and fall great; winter nymphing and March - April midging can be excellent. In May and June, run-off makes the river pretty much unfishable.

Season & Limits
Open year-round.

Accommodations & Services
All services in Big Sky and Bozeman (see appendix). Gallatin Riverguides, (406-995-2290).

Nearby Fly Fishing
So many choices in Montana, so little time.

Rating
For great western freestone fly fishing, a 10.

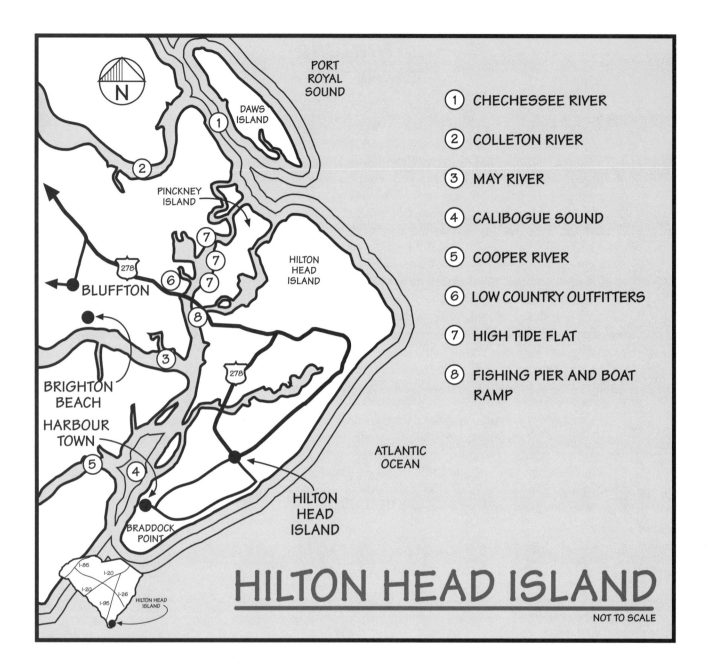

HILTON HEAD ISLAND

1. CHECHESSEE RIVER
2. COLLETON RIVER
3. MAY RIVER
4. CALIBOGUE SOUND
5. COOPER RIVER
6. LOW COUNTRY OUTFITTERS
7. HIGH TIDE FLAT
8. FISHING PIER AND BOAT RAMP

NOT TO SCALE

Wanda Taylor is a fly fishing instructor with over fourteen years of experience. With her husband, Captain Gary Taylor, Wanda owns Taylor & Taylor Fly Fishing Schools. Together they developed a new method of teaching the full spectrum of fly fishing. Wanda is a graduate of the Orvis Guide School, Joan Wulff's School of Fly Fishing, and Lefty Kreh's instructors course. She is also the first woman ever to be certified as a Master Fly Caster by the Federation of Fly Fishers and the first woman endorsed as an Orvis guide in the Southeastern United States. Wanda and Gary are also full-time field representatives for Fly Logic, Inc. They support fly shops, put on fly fishing clinics and demonstrations, and provide technical writing and management for the company.

Hilton Head Island
South Carolina
Wanda Taylor

"The land is healthful ...The ayr is clear and sweet and the country very pleasant and delightful," wrote Captain William Hilton in 1663 after sailing north from Barbados. He described the Hilton River "Low Country" (now the Broad River) and his first sighting of Hilton Head Island.

Hilton Head is awash in the history of the Yemassee Indians and the Revolutionary and Civil Wars, and there is still visible evidence of rice, cotton, and indigo empires built by slaves and the sweat of the common man. To this day, the island maintains a largely nonindustrial economy based on tourism and fishing the bays and estuaries for oysters, clams, and shrimp. These fertile waters provide a constantly replenishing food source for redfish and other species. These waters are also a fly fishing paradise, under-fished and overlooked by many tourists.

For no-nonsense anglers who like to go it on their own, I recommend wading the Low Country's high tide, short grass flats for tailing redfish. Late summer through October, for three or four days during the full and new moon phases, high tides reach 8' and higher, flooding areas of spartina-grass flats that get wet only a few times a year. The roadside grass flats near the Broad River Bridge, Lemon Island, and Pinckney Island (see map #7) are accessible by foot or sea kayak. Always check the tide charts and weather forecast before venturing out to fish.

Late fall through early spring sees another redfish phenomenon—schools of 200 - 300 fish gathered on the island's low tidal flats. The colder water temperatures of winter slow the fish's metabolism. In this "calmer" state, they're a perfect target for fly anglers in guided flats boats. During these months, the best fishing on low tide flats is 2 hours before and 2 hours after low tide.

Located an hour and a half south of Charleston, South Carolina and 45 minutes north of Savannah, Georgia off Interstate 16, Hilton Head Island offers a year-round love affair for fly anglers who will seek the adventures of "The Low Country."

Types of Fish
Surf: Whiting, redfish, pompano, ladyfish, flounder, bluefish.
Inshore: Redfish (Drum or Spots), spotted seatrout, cobia, black drum, flounder, jack crevalle, ladyfish, sheephead, tarpon, bluefish, Spanish mackerel.
Nearshore: King mackerel, false albacore.
Offshore: Dolphin (dorado), grouper, white marlin, wahoo, sailfish, red snapper, blue marlin.

Known Baitfish
Shrimp, fiddler crab, mullet, mud minnows, silver sides, menhaden.

Equipment to Use
Rods: 9 foot, 7, 8, or 9 weight.
Reels: Saltwater resistant disc drag.
Lines: Weight forward floating, intermediate clear sink tip, and sinking lines.
Leaders: 9', 12-15 lb. for redfish, wire tippet for toothy fish.
Wading: Neoprene or Gortex waders for winter. Shorts and flats boots for summer.
Boating: Sea kayaks, john boats, flats boats for inshore. Offshore, bigger boats are better for rough seas and big fish.
Other: Sunscreen, bug repellent, striping basket, hat, Polarized sunglasses, fingerless gloves, binoculars, cell phone or VHF radio for emergency.

Flies to Use
Crabs: Cohenour/Lambert Pheasant-Under-Grass, Del's Merkin Crab #2-4. *Shrimp:* patterns with gold flash, as Chris Weber's Rattle Shrimp. *Deceivers:* Lefty's red/white, root beer/white. *Clouser Minnows:* Chartreuse/white, olive/white. *Poppers:* blue/white, red/white. Bonefish flies, Seaducers in black/white.

When to Fish
365 days a year there is a species to fish for, and there are various seasons. Redfish is prime January - December.

Seasons & Limits
Nonresident saltwater license, $5.50 if fishing from private boat. No license required for fishing from land or with a guide.

Accommodations & Services
Renowned for lodging and food. See Appendix for listing.

Rating
Beauty and variety of salt water fishing, a definite 9 or 10.

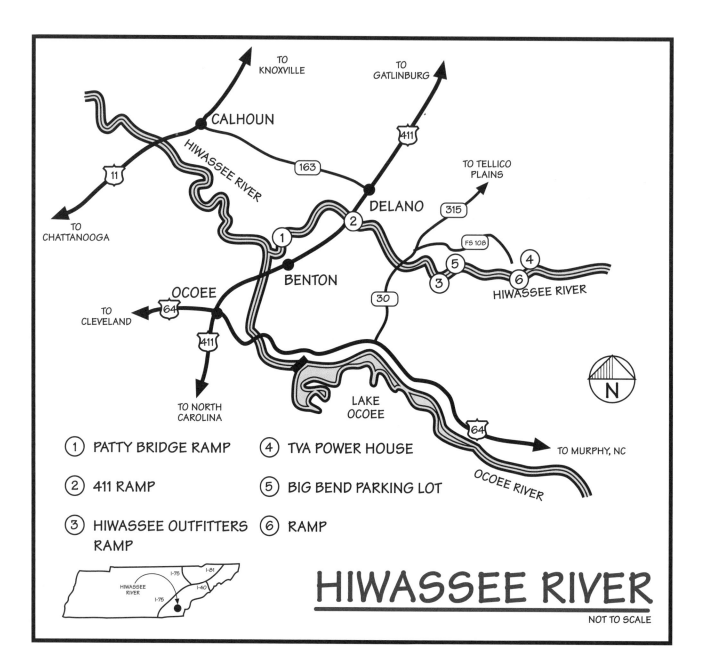

1. PATTY BRIDGE RAMP
2. 411 RAMP
3. HIWASSEE OUTFITTERS RAMP
4. TVA POWER HOUSE
5. BIG BEND PARKING LOT
6. RAMP

HIWASSEE RIVER

NOT TO SCALE

Wanda Taylor is the female half of a nationally recognized husband and wife team of fly fishing instructors and guides. With husband, Captain Gary Taylor, Wanda owns Taylor & Taylor Fly Fishing Schools. Her strong communication skills, leadership, and contagious sense of humor encourage people to exceed their expectations in the art of fly fishing. Gary and Wanda are also field representatives for Fly Logic, Inc. She is currently an active member of TU, FFF, Georgia Women Fly Fishers, founding Board Member of the Tennessee Brookies, and assists with the TWRA's "Beyond Becoming an Outdoor Woman" program as well as "Casting for Recovery," a program for women recovering from breast cancer.

Hiwassee River
Tennessee
Wanda Taylor

John Muir loved the Hiwassee River so much that he established a trail along its banks in the late 1800's.   In his journal, he wrote, "Such a river the Hiwassee with its surface broken to a thousand gems, and its forest walls vine-draped and flowery, as Eden.   And how fine the song it sings."   Today, like the legendary explorer and naturalist, novice as well as seasoned anglers journey to the Hiwassee every year for some of the finest fly fishing in the east.   They know that a well presented fly will often entice a rainbow or brown trout from the depths of the Hiwassee's emerald waters.

The Hiwassee River is a tailwater regulated by the Tennessee Valley Authority.   The river has three, approximately five-mile-long sections.   All three sections are "put and take," but most anglers practice catch and release.   Except for the trophy trout, upper section from Big Bend Recreation Site to the L & N Railroad bridge in Reliance, most of the river is accessible from the road. The middle section runs from Reliance through high cliffs to the Highway 411 bridge.   Remains of Cherokee fish traps still exist in Reliance and at Gee Creek Campground.

The lower section begins at the Highway 411 bridge and flows by private homes and farms to either the new Patty Bridge takeout or the Two Rivers Campground a mile further downstream where the Ocoee and Hiwassee converge.   This lower section fishes best in the early spring.

The Hiwassee has deep pools and limestone rock formations and should be treated with extreme caution even when the river is "off" and wadeable.   When the river is "on," a water craft is needed.   Float tubes, canoes, kayaks, rafts, and drift boats are all used, but float tubes are not recommended from Big Bend to the L & N Railroad takeout.   The TVA records a water flow schedule each day after 6 in the evening.   You can receive this information by calling 1-800-238-2264.

To reach the headwaters of the Hiwassee, travel Highway 411 north from Benton, and then take a right on Highway 30.   Continue to Reliance, where you need to take a left at the bridge crossing the river.   At the end of the bridge, make a right onto Forest Service Road 108 which ends at the Appalachian power house.

Types of Fish
Rainbows and browns.

Known Hatches
This river has late hatches, so sleep in and fish late.

Equipment to Use
Rods: 9 foot, 5 or 6 weight.
Reels: Disc drag to match rod.
Lines: Weight forward, floating.
Leaders: 9 to 12 feet, 5 to 7X.
Wading & Boating: Chest waders, boots and wading staff are a must. Newcomers should hire a guide if they intend to float the river.

Flies to Use
Standard dries, nymphs, and streamers will always work.   Check with area shops for local favorites.

When to Fish
Best from April through July.   Nymphs in the morning hours always work.   When hatches begin coming off, change to the appropriate dry fly. Mayflies fly in May, so be here!

Seasons & Limits
Fish year-round.   Trophy trout from Big Bend to L&N railroad bridge. Artificial lures only, limit two, 14" or longer per day.   Other areas, 7 trout a day per angler. Check regulations.

Accommodations & Services
There are a variety of lodges, outfitters, and fly shops nearby.   See the appendix for a listing.

Nearby Fly Fishing
Tributary streams: Wolf, Smith, Big Lost Creeks and the Gee,
Tellico and Clinch Rivers. Great Smokey Mt. National Park.

Rating
April - July a 10. August - February, a 5.

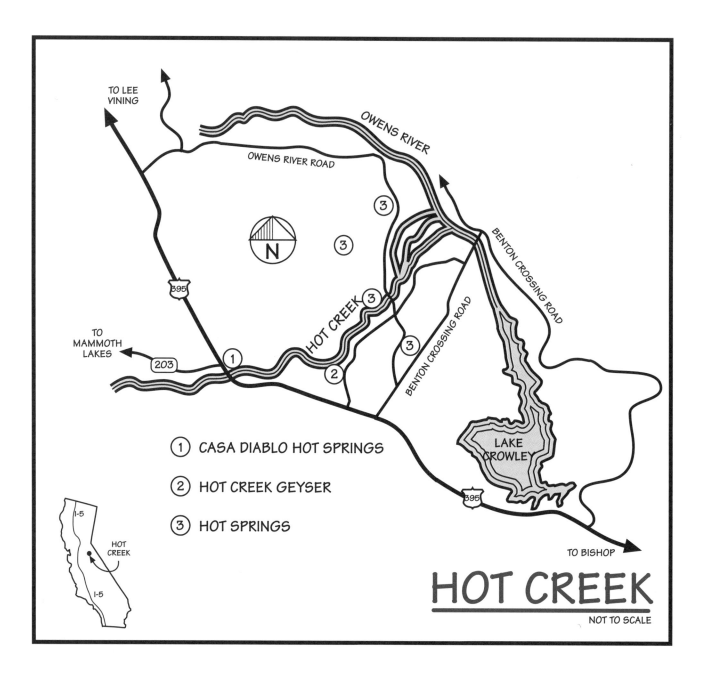

1 CASA DIABLO HOT SPRINGS

2 HOT CREEK GEYSER

3 HOT SPRINGS

HOT CREEK

NOT TO SCALE

Cheryl Hoey's father taught her to fish, the source of their only conflict. Her father kept fish . . . she refused to, the perfect release occurring at some moment after her father saw her playing a fish and before he could reach her with his net. Today, Cheryl manages the San Francisco Orvis store and has the opportunity to fish in some very special places, but Hot Creek remains her favorite. Her daughter, Leslie, caught her first fish on Hot Creek, and Cheryl married a nice fellow named Jack who happened to be with them for that special moment. After all, he not only nets the fish for her . . . he also lets them go!

Hot Creek
California
Cheryl Hoey

*H*ot Creek is often called the most productive stream in the western United States. Various statistics support this claim, but the evidence most often cited is from a California Department of Fish and Game electroshock survey that counted 11,000 fish per mile—a remarkable number, for such a narrow creek, 7,000 feet above sea level, and managed entirely as a wild trout water.

Such abundance draws anglers to Hot Creek, but the astounding natural beauty of the area attracts other observers as well. The stream carves a deep canyon through an active geothermal area just east of the Sierra Nevada. Puffs of steam rise from the waters edge, and hot springs bubble up from the ground along the trail. These springs gave the creek its name; they also keep the Hot Creek's water temperature between fifty-five and sixty degrees, nurturing abundant plant and insect life, and creating an ideal habitat for trout.

Effectively fishing Hot Creek rarely requires casts of more than twenty feet. Standing on the bank, you can see fish working close by. I emphasize standing on the bank because wading is not only discouraged but also unnecessary, except, at times, to release a fish. Moreover, the creek's fish are not easily spooked and seem unfazed by the presence of anglers. These conditions make Hot Creek an excellent place for beginners to try their luck, but there are times when extremely selective fish, heavy weed growth, and high desert winds combine to challenge even the most skilled angler.

The public section of water between Hot Creek Ranch and the parking area at Owens River Road is approximately two miles long. The Owens River Road end has public restrooms and a paved trail down to the creek. Bathing and swimming areas are located at the foot of the trail, and many tired anglers discover that a warm soak offers the perfect ending to a day of fishing this beautiful small stream.

Types of Fish
Browns and rainbows.

Known Hatches
Baetis, caddis, scuds, ants, and hoppers.

Equipment to Use
Rods: 9 foot, 4 to 6 weight.
Reels: Standard spring and pawl or disc drag.
Lines: Weight forward floating.
Leaders: 9 and 12 foot, 5 to 7X.
Wading: No wading required.

Flies to Use
Dries: Blue winged olive, CDC Caddis, Madam X, hopper, ant, and beetle.
Nymphs: Beadhead Pheasant Tail, scud, and brassie.
Streamers: Black or olive leech pattern.

When to Fish
Because of consistent water temperatures, Hot Creek fishes well all day throughout the season.

Seasons & Limits
Last Saturday in April until October 31st No kill, zero limit.

Accommodations & Services
The Mammoth Lakes area has all necessary hotel, restaurant, banking, and fly shop services (see appendix).

Nearby Fly Fishing
Owens River, Crowley Lake, June Lakes Loop.

Rating
Hot creek provides opportunities for beginners and a challenge for seasoned anglers, a solid 8.

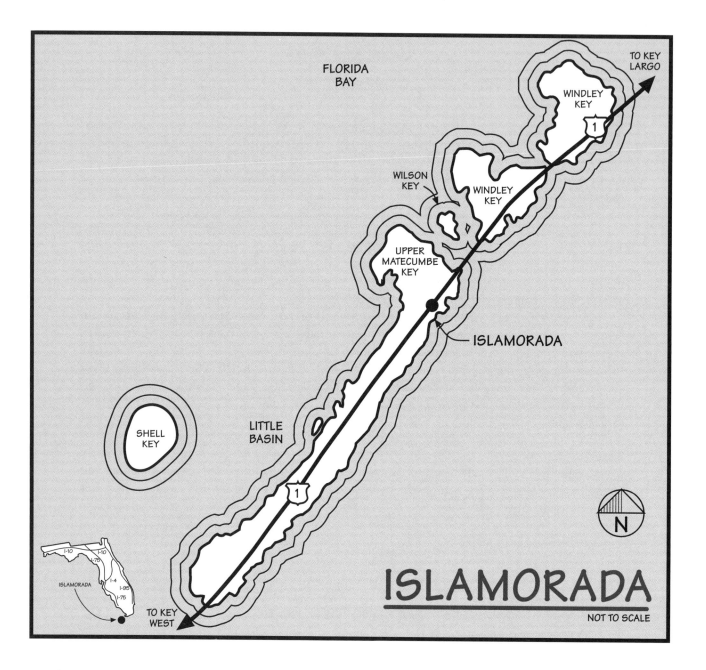

FLORIDA
BAY

TO KEY
LARGO

WINDLEY
KEY

WILSON
KEY

WINDLEY
KEY

UPPER
MATECUMBE
KEY

ISLAMORADA

SHELL
KEY

LITTLE
BASIN

N

ISLAMORADA

NOT TO SCALE

ISLAMORADA

TO KEY
WEST

Jodi Pate grew up in steelhead country, Hood River, Oregon to be exact, but until she met her husband, legendary fly fisherman Billy Pate, ten years ago, she had never fished in her life. Her first fishing experience was for Argentine rainbows and browns, and she quickly proceeded from there to big game fish. Since that time, Jodi has eagerly transformed herself into a capable angler in her own right, currently holding three Pacific sailfish and one black marlin world records. Jodi spearheaded the effort to establish the IGFA world record fly rod categories for women that became effective January of 1997. Her favorite fishing spots are Australia, Costa Rica, and Morocco. She is currently president of International Women Fly Fishers.

Islamorada
Florida
Jodi Pate

*I*magine a school of hundred pound fish in gin-clear, four-foot-deep water swimming right at you! You make your best cast and start to strip. Amazingly, one of these monsters breaks away from the school and suddenly swirls, engulfing your fly. With knees shaking and heart pounding, you set the hook hard again and again. In the shallow flats, the silver king has no place to go but straight up, shaking its head and thrashing the water. Tarpon on a fly . . . is there another fishing experience even remotely like it?

Islamorada, Florida is a prime place for you to jump your first tarpon. Located only an hour and a half's drive south of Miami, Islamorada, like everywhere in the Keys, is, to say the least, very casual, its laid back atmosphere sharply contrasting with the adrenaline rush of its fishing.

Whether you decide to fish for tarpon in the "back country", a series of saltwater lakes and mangrove islands, or in the open water on either the gulf or the Atlantic side of Islamorada, you will need the best guide you can hire with a sixteen-to-eighteen foot flats skiff. With changing wind and tides, your skiff may be "staked out" or constantly moving. In either case, you must be able to cast "around the clock." The guide may say, "You've got fish coming at 11 o'clock!" Remembering that the bow of the skiff always points at 12, you face your body towards 11 o'clock and make your cast.

You don't need to be a tournament caster to fish for Islamorada's tarpon, but you should be able to deliver a 3 or 4/0 tarpon fly up to sixty feet with some accuracy. Your fly must be presented approximately ten feet ahead of the tarpon and within two feet on either side of its path. Then, retrieve slowly with one-foot strips. Also, work at keeping your backcast high. This will minimize the chance of hooking yourself or, more importantly, your guide who stands exposed behind you on the elevated poling platform.

Hooking a tarpon on a fly is one of the sport's truly exhilarating experiences. Hooking one against the beautiful backdrop of Islamorada and the other Florida Keys will be a memory you will treasure for a lifetime.

Types of Fish
Tarpon, permit, bonefish, and barracuda.

Known Baitfish
Mullet, shrimp, pinfish, crabs, and worms.

Equipment to Use
Rods: 9 foot, 11 or 12 weight.
Reels: Any durable saltwater reel capable of holding 200 + yards of 30 lb. backing.
Lines: Weight forward floating or slow sink saltwater lines to match rod.
Leaders: 8 foot with 16 -20 lb. class and 100 lb. shock tippet.
Boating: Tarpon are pursued from a flats skiff or similar craft.
Other: When you head for Islamorada, don't forget 15+ sunblock, hat, protective clothing, deck shoes, polarized sunglasses, snacks and plenty of water. Also, remember that flats skiffs provide little shade and even less in the area of bathroom facilities. I simply grab a bucket and a large beach towel and make the best of it!

Flies to Use
Little Brown Tarpon Fly, crabs, and minnow patterns.

When to Fish
May 1 to July 15th is best.

Season & Limits
All year, no limit, but tarpon are generally not eaten and catch and release is the norm.

Accommodations & Services
There are plenty of hotels/motels, restaurants and services in Islamorada and up and down the Keys.

Nearby Fly Fishing
Islamorada area, offshore—dolphin, sailfish, mackerel, and jacks. Backcountry—tarpon, bonefish, redfish, snook, seatrout, jack crevalle, and ladyfish.

Rating
Tarpon on a fly in the Keys has to rate a 10.

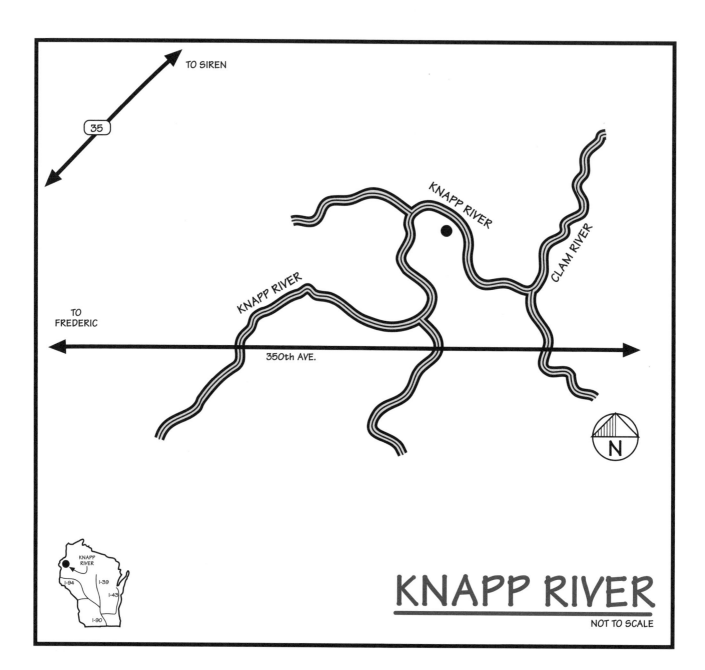

TO SIREN

35

TO
FREDERIC

KNAPP RIVER

KNAPP RIVER

CLAM RIVER

350th AVE.

N

KNAPP
RIVER

I-94

I-39

I-43

I-90

KNAPP RIVER

NOT TO SCALE

Nancy Jobe began fishing at the age of five with a willow branch, a stretch of line, and a glob of leftover Fig Newton. The three-pound large mouth Nancy landed on that rudimentary set up hooked her on fishing for life. She began fly fishing nine years ago and has since become an FFF Certified Casting Instructor, a founding member of The Minnesota Women's Fly Fishing Club, and a board member of the International Festival of Women Fly Fishers. Nancy lives near Minneapolis with her husband and two children and is currently finishing a book on fishing, My Angels Have Fins.

Knapp River
Wisconsin
Nancy Willette Jobe

A bit of history and nostalgia await you in Lewis, Wisconsin. Here you can fish the Knapp River and stay at Seven Pines Lodge as Calvin Coolidge did when he visited in 1928. And remember *The Way of the Trout*? It was filmed on the section of the Knapp controlled by the lodge that holds stocked and native rainbows, browns, and brookies.

A rustic secluded setting of tall pines and a variety of water conditions make the Knapp River the perfect setting for fly anglers of all skill levels. Each new section or turn of the river gives you the captivating feeling of fishing your own, personal stream. The river has been well maintained with appropriate fish structure, offering areas of sunny embankments and shaded overhangs as well as an open pond area perfect for casting practice or fishing without catching "tree trout."

A well-presented, drag-free dry fly or nymph will almost always draw the attention of a feisty rainbow or brown. As with any stream, the fish get a bit spooky toward the end of August and September. Use this time to work on approach and presentation skills.

The Knapp River and lodge are about 80 miles northeast of Minneapolis/St. Paul. Take Interstate 35 north, then east on Minnesota Highway 70, and then south on Wisconsin Highway 35 When you reach Lewis, Wisconsin, turn left on Main Street, go one block to 115th Street, drive to 340th Avenue and turn left. Seven Pines Lodge is the first driveway on the right.

The lodge offers unique accommodations on the Knapp River and guests receive complimentary fishing. If you don't want to stay at the lodge or are just fishing for the day, access can be purchased. But, whether you stay a week or a day, you will be enchanted, as I was, by this beautiful and unique fishery.

Types of Fish
Rainbows, browns, and brookies.

Known Hatches
Baetis, Tricorythodes (Tricos), Hexagenias, various species of Emphemerella, and others.

Equipment to Use
Rods: 8 to 9 foot, 4 to 7 weight.
Reels: Click or disc to match rod.
Lines: Double taper or weight forward floating. Distance casting is not necessary.
Leaders: 7 to 12 foot, 4 to 6X.
Wading: Waders, boots with felt and cleats. This stream can be very slippery with bottom vegetation in almost all areas.

Flies to Use
Dries: Blue winged olive #16-18, blue and mahogany dun, Light Hendrickson, sulphur, light cahill #14-16, March brown, Gray Fox, Brown Drake #12, hexes and Green drake #8-14, white or gray-winged Trico #18-20 fished wet.
Nymphs: Nymph of the above, brassie #20, tan, brown, olive scud, Hare's Ear #14-16, Pheasant Tail #14-12, Peeking Caddis #16-18.
Streamers: Black, brown, and olive Wooly Bugger.

When to Fish
Best times are morning, 6 to 9 a.m. and evening, 4 to 8 p.m.

Seasons & Limits
March 1st to Sept. 30th, catch & release, single, barbless hook. Wisconsin fishing license and trout stamp required.

Accommodations & Services
Seven Pines Lodge's (see appendix) scenic, north-woods setting is by far my favorite (715-653-2323). Four-course meals and fishing access. Numerous other hotels & motels 30-40 minutes away.

Nearby Fly Fishing
Other productive streams in western Wisconsin include the Rush, Willow, and Kinnickinnic rivers. All are close enough to the Knapp so you may want to try them all!

Rating
Late season fishing is hard, a 6. Early season the Knapp is an 8 due to the ease of catching many fish.

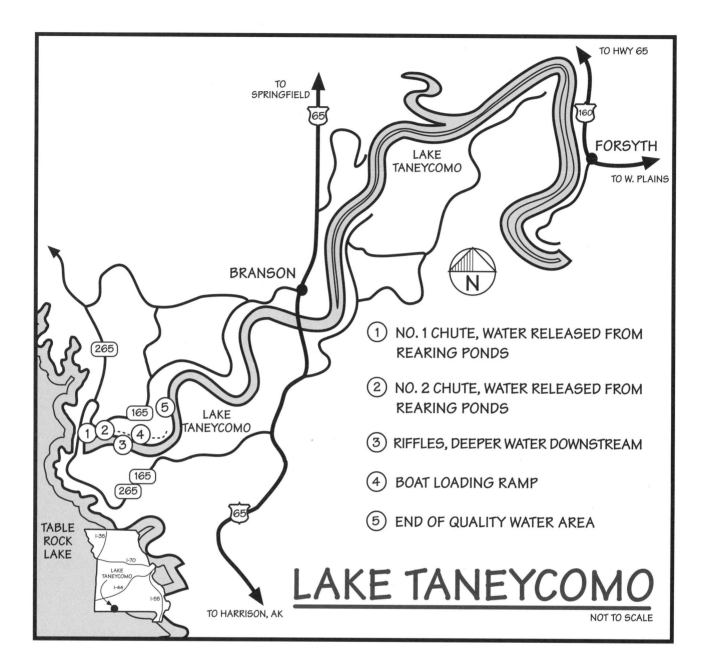

1. NO. 1 CHUTE, WATER RELEASED FROM REARING PONDS

2. NO. 2 CHUTE, WATER RELEASED FROM REARING PONDS

3. RIFFLES, DEEPER WATER DOWNSTREAM

4. BOAT LOADING RAMP

5. END OF QUALITY WATER AREA

LAKE TANEYCOMO

NOT TO SCALE

Carolyn Parker has been fishing almost all her life but became seriously interested in fly fishing over fifteen years ago on Lake Taneycomo. She has since fished many of the streams and rivers throughout the western states and Alaska where each water resulted in a new experience, a new technique, a new fly, and usually a wonderful new friend or friends who shared her passion for fly fishing. Carolyn and her husband retired early from the "management world." They now operate River Run Outfitters, a fly shop in Branson, Missouri, where they guide, tie flies, build rods, and look for new, exciting waters to fish.

Lake Taneycomo
Missouri
Carolyn Parker

*T*he White River wanders through some of the most beautiful scenery this country has to offer. In the spring, the Ozark Mountains in southwest Missouri are covered with cherry blossoms and flowering dogwood. The summer months bring lush, green foliage, and fall is full of the fiery oranges, reds, and yellows of hard oaks. Would it surprise you, then, to hear that my favorite time of the year is winter? It wouldn't if you knew of my passion for fishing, and winter is prime time for fly fishing the section of White River along the town of Branson, Missouri known as Lake Taneycomo.

Impounded by Table Rock Dam on one end and Power Site Dam on the other, Lake Taneycomo stretches 23 miles and has long been a popular fishing destination. So popular, in fact, new regulations for the lake were implemented March, 1997. The area from the dam down to Fall Creek is catch and release with a slot size of 12 -20". Only flies or artificial lures are allowed in this stretch of water (approx. 3 miles). Recently it was not uncommon to catch several fish in the 18 - 20" range with some even larger trophies. Fishing below this area is also good but, for the most part, requires a boat. Fly rod fishing with micro jigs along the banks in 6 - 7' of water is productive in the lower part of the lake.

The most accessible wading area is the first mile and a half just below Table Rock Dam. As with any tailwater, watch for water releases. The river can rise rapidly depending on the number of units in operation. Listen for a horn which the water master usually blows once for each unit he is getting ready to release. A safe practice is to head for the bank as soon as you hear the first horn, so you're not cut off from dry ground.

Types of Fish
Rainbows, browns, and cuttbows. Lower lake has some crappie and bass during the summer.

Known Hatches
Mayflies and midges.

Equipment to Use
Rods: 7 to 9 foot, 4 to 6 weight.
Reels: Click or disc drag to match rod.
Lines: Double taper or weight forward floating and sinking.
Leaders: 6 to 10 foot, 5 or 6X.
Wading & Boating: Easy wading below dam, use waders and boots, hippers OK. A boat or float tube works well.

Flies to Use
Dries: Elk Hair Caddis, Griffith's Gnat, Light Cahill, Parachute Adams, terrestrial, especially grasshopper.
Nymphs: Hare's Ear and green or yellow floss bodied soft hackle, Red Ass, brown or gray scud #14-16, small, green or copper emerger #16-22.
Streamers: Olive, black or brown Wooly Bugger, sculpin patterns (especially at night) #10-14. *Other:* White, black, yellow, moss green jig, less than 1/100 of an ounce.

When to Fish
Spring, fall, winter best. Fish summer during early a.m., late p.m. and at night.

Seasons & Limits
Open all year. Trout limit five per day, ten in possession. Slot limit in water below the dam. Check current regulations.

Accommodations & Services
KOA campground one mile south of Table Rock Dam on Highway 165. City campground in downtown Branson right on the lake. Motels, cabins, all other services in Branson. River Run Outfitters, (877-699-FISH).

Nearby Fly Fishing
Tailwaters: Beaver, Taneycomo, and Bull Shoals are within 2 hours of each other. Table Rock and Bull Shoals lakes for bass, crappie, walleye, other game fish. Check flows in Taneycomo and Beaver first, (417-336-5083).

Rating
I find it hard not to give Lake Taneycomo a 9.

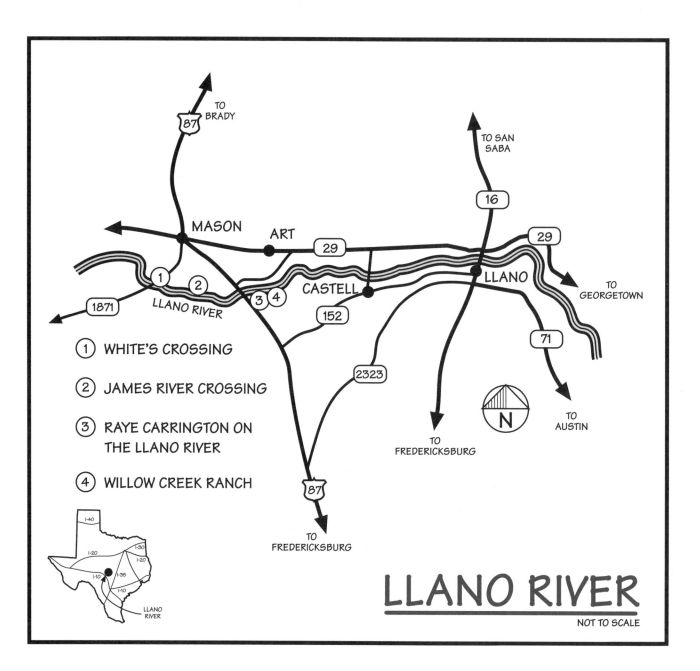

1 WHITE'S CROSSING

2 JAMES RIVER CROSSING

3 RAYE CARRINGTON ON
THE LLANO RIVER

4 WILLOW CREEK RANCH

LLANO RIVER

NOT TO SCALE

Raye Carrington had an epiphany twenty years ago, when she was learning to cast. She found the act of throwing a fly line so magical that catching fish became secondary. Fly fishing has since enriched Raye's life in many ways. She's edited a book of fishing quotations, written a history of a Colorado trout club, and collaborated on Fish and Whistle, *a musical tale performed for thousands of Texas school children. Raye is an FFF Certified Casting Instructor and a member of the G. Loomis Pro Staff. Recently her dream has really come true with the opening of her inn, Raye Carrington on the Llano River.*

Llano River
Texas
Raye Carrington

Texas does have a few remaining wild rivers, and the spring-fed Llano is one of them. This spectacular fishery flows through West Texas ranch country and empties into the Colorado River. The clean, dry air of rocky, cactus and mesquite-covered hills is a perfect match for the sparkling river.

The Llano's crystal-clear waters are home to the graceful, native Guadalupe bass. They share the river with spotted and largemouth bass, catfish, sunfish, gar, and carp. Like trout, Guadalupe bass hang out in the river's faster water. When this water gets cold, a heavily-weighted fly may be needed to reach the bottom of a run. But even on cold days, dry flies often tempt bass and perch to the surface. I've caught some nice largemouth in quiet water using a huge Royal Wulff that was tied for steelhead. I've also had very good luck with a Clouser Crayfish, especially around rocks.

I use a six weight most of the time I fish the Llano. I think it handles the combination of wind and heavy or bulky flies a bit better than a lighter rod. A more delicate rod will work, but you'll have to work harder. Floating lines are also the norm on this river. When the water temperature drops, an extra spool with a medium sink rate or sink-tip line can come in handy.

The river has been designated a navigable stream meaning anglers in or on the water are considered on public land. Nevertheless, landowners along the river take a dim view of trespassers. If you ask, you'll often be allowed access. There's enough current to make paddling interesting and enough quiet, deep water to hold the plentiful perch and largemouth.

Fortunately, there are several convenient public access points along the Llano for boats or wade fishermen; the crossings at the James River and at the tiny town of Castell are my favorites. Once you are in the water, you can sometimes wade for several miles. This is mostly easy as the river rolls over solid granite and limestone rock with an occasional sand or gravel bar. Wet wading is comfortable from about April until the first freeze in the later part of October or November.

Types of Fish
Guadalupe, spotted, and largemouth bass, catfish, sunfish, gar and carp.

Known Hatches or Bait
Mayfly hatches almost all year, snails and leeches.

Equipment to Use
Rods: 9 foot, 6 weight.
Reels: Click or disc to match rod.
Lines: Weight forward floating, medium sink, and sink-tip.
Leaders: 7 to 9 foot, 3 to 5X.
Wading & Boating: Neoprene waders in cool months. Wet wade warm months. Perfect canoe or kayak water.

Flies to Use
Dries: Popper, Madame X, other large drys.
Nymphs: Heavily-weighted mayfly, damsel fly.
Streamers: Sparsely-tied Clouser Minnow #4-10, Charlie Cypert's Mylar Minnow, Ninny Bug. Black, olive Wooly Bugger #4-12, leech, Clouser Crayfish.

When to Fish
Fish year long, especially sunny winter days. Fish are more active March - November.

Season & Limits
Fishing allowed year round. Five bass per day (any combination), minimum 14" for largemouth, 12" for Guadalupe and spotted bass. No limit on panfish. I recommend catch & release. Don't forget a license!

Accommodations & Services
Towns of Mason and Llano for motels, B&B's, services and restaurants. Two small, rustic inns south of Mason off Highway 87 have river access (one being mine, see appendix). Public and private camping nearby. Mason and Llano for popular BBQ: nothing fancy, just fabulous slow-cooked meats served on butcher paper with sides of frijoles, potato salad, coleslaw and dessert. Towns have web sites for information.

Rating
Beautiful fish in a beautiful Texas setting. A solid 10.

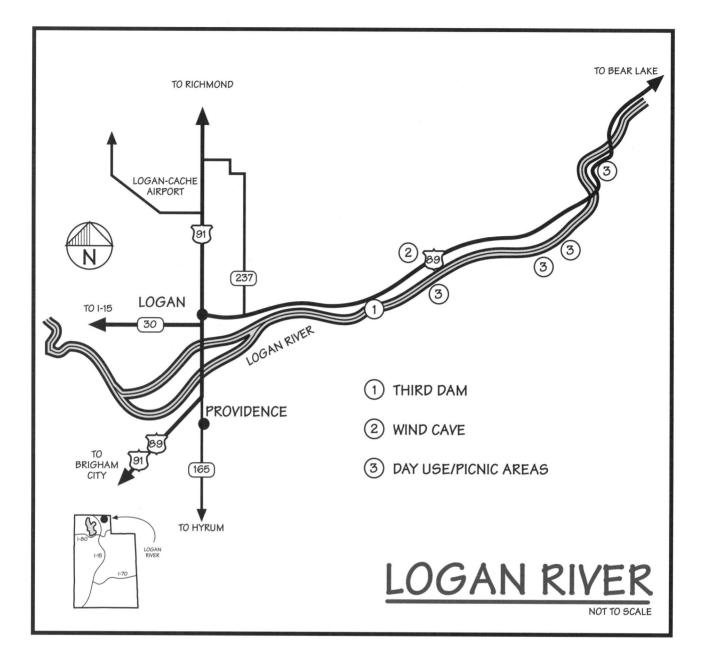

TO RICHMOND

TO BEAR LAKE

LOGAN-CACHE AIRPORT

N

91

237

TO I-15

LOGAN

30

LOGAN RIVER

89

1

3

2

89

3

3

3

PROVIDENCE

89

91

TO BRIGHAM CITY

165

TO HYRUM

1 THIRD DAM

2 WIND CAVE

3 DAY USE/PICNIC AREAS

I-80

LOGAN RIVER

I-15

I-70

LOGAN RIVER

NOT TO SCALE

Rainy Riding began fly fishing at the age of five. In 1971, having never tied a fly in her life, she taught her first fly tying class after learning two patterns only a half hour before the class started. The two new patterns per week she had to learn to stay ahead of that first class has grown into Rainy's Flies and Supplies. This very successful retail fly shop and mail order business features an array of specialty fly tying products and tools as well as highly effective fly patterns, especially her foam terrestrials. Rainy currently resides in Logan, Utah with her four children.

Logan River
Utah
Rainy Riding

*A*fter our first fly fishing lesson, we retired to the bank of the Logan River and warmed our numb feet on the large limestone boulders that radiated the warmth of the sun. Water dripped from our legs, leaving puddles as we discussed the art and science of fly fishing. And so, the Logan taught a few more angling lessons as it has over the years, molding so many novices into fine fly fishers.

The Logan is an average size river nestled at the bottom of the steep ridges of Logan Canyon. Its headwaters are home to the threatened Bonneville cutthroat and the occasional brookie, and its frequent steep gradients can make for difficult wading for the inexperienced or unaware. There are plenty of safely wadeable stretches, but know your limits as there are some dangerous places where judgment and extreme caution are mandatory.

Logan River trout average 5 - 10" with larger fish common. Browns, rainbows, cutthroat, and the occasional mountain whitefish inhabit the lower and middle sections of the river, while cutthroat inhabit the smaller, boulder-strewn, pocket water of the upper stretches.

As on most challenging trout water, drag-free drifts on the Logan are a must! Dead drift dry flies or nymphs, up or downstream. Properly fished wet flies can arouse aggressive or curious trout, and the river's deeper holes are effectively fished with a deep nymph tandem, rigged with enough weight to sink the flies in faster water. The Logan offers frequent and valuable lessons on mending and line control.

Logan, Utah is approximately 90 miles north of Salt Lake City. From Logan take Highway 89 which parallels the river as it winds its way through the approximately 27 mile canyon, ending at Bear Lake in Garden City, Utah.

Types of Fish
Browns, rainbows, cutthroat, and mountain whitefish with the occasional brookie on the upper Logan.

Know Hatches & Baitfish
Green, gray, and brown drakes, blue winged olives, pale morning duns, and other mayflies. Golden and winter stoneflies, midges, various caddis and the occasional sculpin.

Equipment to Use
Rods: 8 to 9 foot, 3 to 5 weight.
Reels: Click or disc drag to match rod.
Lines: Weight forward or double taper floating.
Leaders: 7 to 9 foot, 4 to 6X.
Wading: Felt soled boots an advantage, studs optional. Neoprene waders for winter, lightweight waders for summer.

Flies to Use
Dries: Mayfly imitation depending on the time of year. Elk and deer hair caddis, other caddis imitations, green drake, golden stonefly, hopper, other attractor and emerger pattern.
Nymphs: Beadhead Hare's Ear, Pheasant Tail, small stonefly, caddis, mayfly.

When to Fish
Winter is good and best in February. Spring fishing can be outstanding until run-off April - May - June. July or August, fishing excellent. Nymph fall - early winter.

Season & Limits
Check Utah Proclamation before fishing!

Accommodations & Services
Campgrounds throughout the canyon with one small motel approximately 7 miles from Logan. Many hotels and other services in the Logan area.

Nearby Fly Fishing
Little Bear River, Blacksmith Fork, Bear River.

Rating
Good variety of water and fish in a beautiful canyon! Has to be an 8.

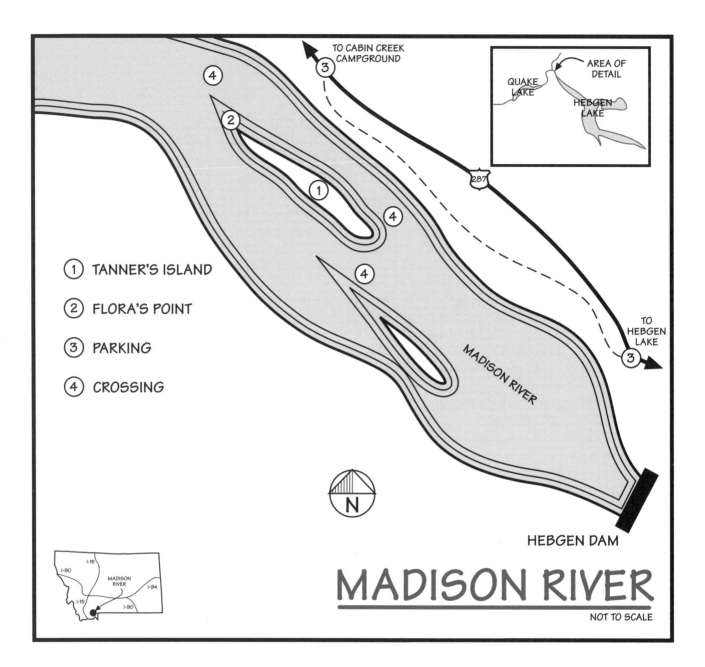

1. TANNER'S ISLAND
2. FLORA'S POINT
3. PARKING
4. CROSSING

TO CABIN CREEK
CAMPGROUND

AREA OF DETAIL

QUAKE LAKE

HEBGEN LAKE

287

TO HEBGEN LAKE

MADISON RIVER

N

HEBGEN DAM

MADISON RIVER

NOT TO SCALE

I-15
I-90
MADISON RIVER
I-94
I-15
I-90

Sally I. Stoner began fishing for bluegill when she was only two-years-old. Six years later, she was pursuing trout on the pristine creeks of the eastern slope of the Sierra Nevada, and loving every minute of it. It was inevitable, perhaps, that she would eventually pick up a fly rod. Stoner is a traveler, teacher, and self-described poet/angler. A fly fishing instructor for the Becoming an Outdoors Women program in California and a Charter Member of the International Women Fly Fishers, Stoner writes for San Luis Obispo Magazine. *Her stories have also appeared in* A Different Angle *and* California Flyfisher.

Madison River
Montana
Sally I. Stoner

As the Madison River tails out below Montana's Hebgen Dam, it is both astonishingly beautiful and enticingly productive for anglers of every skill level. It's here below the dam that the Madison sings most sweetly.

Guarded by mountains and lined with tall evergreens, this section is wide and clear with lots of gravel bars, pocket water, sandy beaches, small islands, boulder falls and great "hidey-holes" for the river's healthy trout. A sturdy population of whitefish is also ready to crash a drag-free nymph. Here, the beginner and expert angler can fish side-by-side with success.

Almost every fly fishing technique can be used here. Mid-June - July, there is an abundance of aquatic insects for fly anglers to imitate. Purists can cast a dry fly upstream to rising trout, and the less fussy can drift a Beadhead Hare's Ear with an indicator. A quirky little nymph, the Serendipity, was invented here. In June a red Serendipity is the fly of choice.

Wading the Madison is difficult if the flows are high. Cross with a wading staff and a partner. Fishing the Highway 287 side is very productive, but watch your backcast for brush and trees. Tanner's Island, the long, narrow, grassy land projection upstream of the Madison's swooping left turn is usually accessible from down river at Flora's Point. Both sides of the island are very fishable. Cast along the boulders on the highway side, and be ready for the golden flash of a big brown.

To reach this section of the Madison from West Yellowstone, take Highway 191 north, turn left on 287. Drive the length of Hebgen Lake. Past the dam, the road curves right, then left across Cabin Creek. From Idaho, travel East on Highway 20, turning left on 87. Take scenic Raynolds Pass and watch for antelope. Cross the Madison, turn right on 287 and climb the gap past the landslide, Quake Lake, and Beaver Creek.

Types of Fish
Rainbows, browns, cuttbows, and mountain whitefish.

Known Hatches
Caddis, mayflies, stoneflies, salmon flies, midges, beetles, worms, grasshoppers, and mosquitoes.

Equipment to Use
Rods: 8 to 9 foot, 4 or 5 weight.
Reels: Click or disc to match rod.
Lines: Weight forward floating.
Leaders: Dries - 9 foot tapered, 3 to 5X. Nymphs - 9 foot, 4 to 5X. Use neon colored poly yarn tied to the butt section with a slip knot for an indicator. Try a small nymph 12" below a #12-14 dry. Check leader every few casts.
Wading: Neoprene waders early summer and evening. Late summer, wet wade.
Other: Hat, sunscreen, polarized glasses.

Flies to Use
Dries: Stimulator, Elk Hair Caddis, Adams, Humpy, Wulff.
Nymphs: Red, olive, and brown Serendipity, Gold Ribbed Hare's Ear, Beadhead Pheasant Tail, San Juan Worm, Prince, caddis pupae, sparkle pupae.

When to Fish
All day in July. Other months best 10 a.m. to 1 p.m. then from 7 p.m. to dark.

Season & Limits
Consult a current edition of Montana fishing regulations.

Accommodations & Services
Campfire Lodge, cabins, campsites with full hook-ups, small store and a café. Camping at Cabin and Beaver Creek, various lodging on Hebgen Lake and Slide Inn. West Yellowstone, 30 miles away, for complete services, including medical clinic.

Nearby Fly Fishing
Hebgen, Henry's and Quake lakes, Cabin, Grayling, Duck and Beaver creeks, Madison Arm and West Fork, Henry's Fork, Gallatin, Taylor's Fork, Firehole and Yellowstone rivers.

Rating
A magic place of fishing adventures. Not a catch & release section, however, and many native fish are killed, a 6.

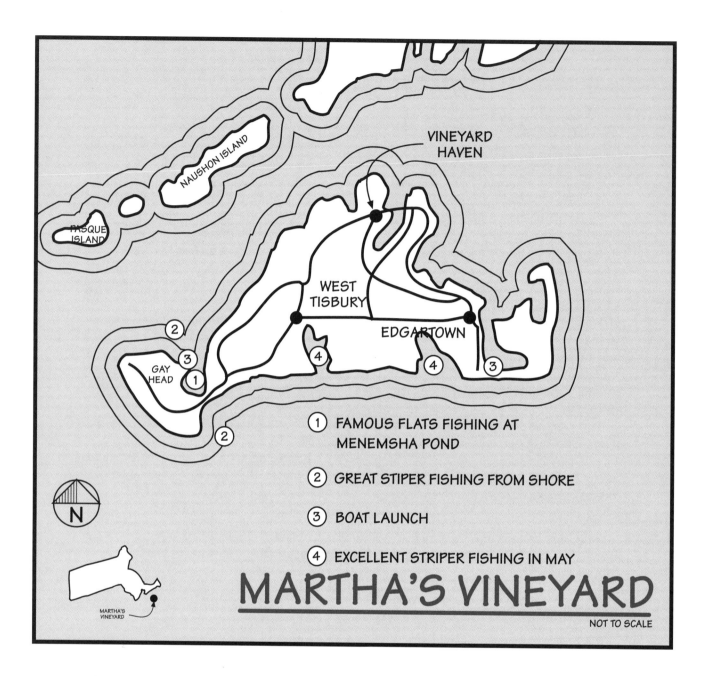

VINEYARD HAVEN

NAUSHON ISLAND

TASQUE ISLAND

WEST TISBURY

EDGARTOWN

② ③ ① GAY HEAD

② ④ ④ ③

N

MARTHA'S VINEYARD

① FAMOUS FLATS FISHING AT MENEMSHA POND

② GREAT STIPER FISHING FROM SHORE

③ BOAT LAUNCH

④ EXCELLENT STRIPER FISHING IN MAY

MARTHA'S VINEYARD

NOT TO SCALE

Page Rogers began fly fishing for trout with her dad, along the brush-lined creeks of Connecticut. Her family has owned land on Martha's Vineyard for four generations, and she has fished the surf and ponds there all her life. Page began tying saltwater flies in 1975, eventually becoming the first woman tier contracted by Umpqua Feather Merchants. Her instructional videos are part of the Hooked on Fly Tying *series and her flies have been featured in many articles and books. Page enjoys sharing her passion for fishing and fly tying with others, especially children in the "Fly Fisher Apprentice Program" based in Ithaca, New York.*

Martha's Vineyard
Massachusetts
Page Rogers

Part of the Elizabeth Island chain, Martha's Vineyard is a 100 square mile island off the southeast coast of Cape Cod. The winter population of 12,000 explodes to 100,000 during summertime.

Deposits of glacial moraine formed the island's higher ground or "up island" during the Pleistocene epoch. As the ice sheet melted, water flowed southward to the sea, forming the outwash plains and network of salt ponds to the east and along the south shore of the island. These salt ponds are the unique key to the island's outstanding sport fishing, serving as incubators for baitfish and crustaceans, providing an endless source of forage for game fish.

Martha's Vineyard offers a wide variety of fly fishing experiences, all within a small geographical area. The beaches are largely pure sand protected by the mainland or other islands, making wading (surf fishing) easy and relatively safe. The largest surf exists on the south shore, and caution should be exercised when fishing there. After the plovers have fledged, the fishing spots along Chappaquiddick or "Chappy," as it is known, is accessed by 4-WD vehicles or boat.

The Vineyard's flats are "deep flats," comfortably poled but not waded. Most flats are within the island's salt ponds. The entire "Middle Flat" area, North, North East of the Edgartown light, provides anglers an excellent opportunity to sight fish to striped bass.

Accessed by boat, the large and powerful tidal rips on both the east and west side of Martha's Vineyard provide action for all the inshore species in season. Often a "bubble" from the Gulfstream will provide action 3 - 10 miles off shore. Schools of yellowfin and bluefin tuna as well as white marlin are regular visitors to these waters.

Many of Martha's Vineyard's vistas are breathtakingly beautiful, and the island's waters are extraordinarily clear and teeming with gamefish. With golf, swimming, shopping, kayaking, and bicycling, there's also plenty to amuse non-angling friends and family.

Types of Fish
Inshore: Striped bass, bluefish, Atlantic bonito, little tunny (false albacore), Spanish mackerel. *Offshore:* Blue shark, white marlin, dorado, skipjack, blue and yellowfin tuna.

Known Baitfish
Sand eels, squid, clam worms, silversides, Atlantic herring, mackerel, green crabs, and lady crabs.

Equipment to Use
Rods: Inshore, 9 to 10', 7 - 10 wt. Offshore, 9', 10 - 14 wt.
Reels: Inshore, direct drive, disc drag, 250 yds. 45 lb. backing. Offshore, direct drive or anti-reverse, disc drag, 500 yds. 80 lb. backing.
Lines: Weight forward floating, clear intermediate sinking, lead-core heads, 250-550 grain.
Leaders: Non-tapered, 20 lb. mono. Wire tippets for bluefish, Spanish mackerel, sharks.
Wading & Boating: Neoprene waders, waterproof jacket. Canoe or kayak in flats and channels.
Other: Polarized sunglasses, bug juice, stripping basket, chest/waist pack, gloves.

Flies to Use
Clouser Deep Minnow, Rogers' Velvet Cinderworm, Big Eye Baitfish, Beach Glass & Slim Jim, Deceiver, Page's Sand Eel, Boyle's Bonito Bunnies, Bob's Banger.

When to Fish
Striped bass, April - Nov. Bluefish, May - Oct. Atlantic bonito, July - Oct. False albacore, Aug. - Oct. Spanish mackerel, Aug. - Sept. Offshore, June to mid-Sept.

Seasons & Limits
Striped bass, 1 per day, 28" min. Bluefish, 10 per day. No limits on other inshore species.

Accommodations & Services
Variety of hotels, rentals, fly shops, boat launches, food, services (see appendix).

Nearby Fly Fishing
Just a 15 minute boat ride to the other islands.

Rating
Great fly fishing in a beautiful, New England setting, a 10.

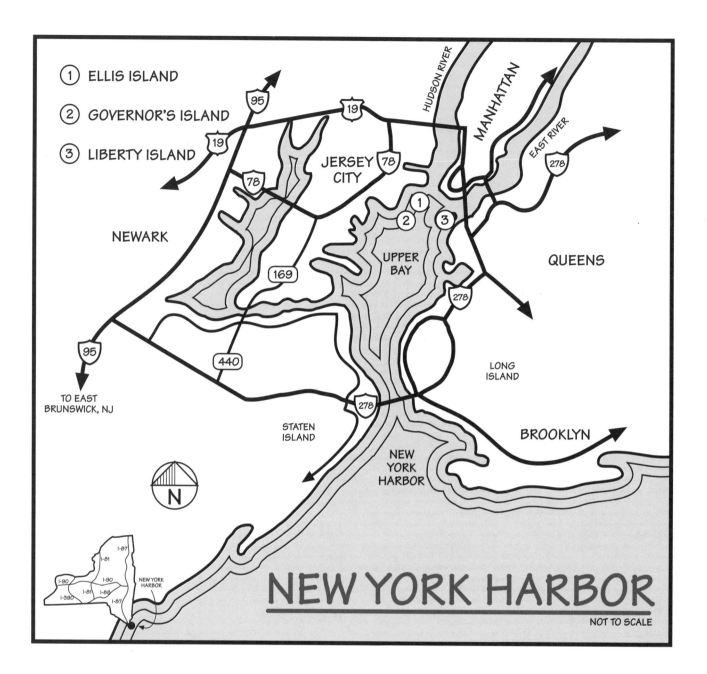

1 ELLIS ISLAND

2 GOVERNOR'S ISLAND

3 LIBERTY ISLAND

HUDSON RIVER

MANHATTAN

EAST RIVER

95

19

19

78

JERSEY CITY

78

NEWARK

169

1

2

3

UPPER BAY

QUEENS

278

95

440

TO EAST BRUNSWICK, NJ

278

LONG ISLAND

STATEN ISLAND

278

NEW YORK HARBOR

BROOKLYN

N

I-87

I-81

I-90

I-90

I-81

I-390

I-88

I-87

NEW YORK HARBOR

NEW YORK HARBOR

NOT TO SCALE

A member of the Theodore Gordon Flyfishers for twenty-six years, Joan Stoliar was the first woman elected to its Board of Directors and is currently Director of their Trout in the Classroom program. A free-lance book designer of many years, her list of credits includes Jonathan Livingston Seagull *and* The Dettes: A Catskill Legend *with many other books on fly fishing in between. Joan formed Willowkill Press with Eric Leiser and Larry Solomon for the express purpose of celebrating the Dettes, founders of the Catskill school of fly tying. She is also the founder of Fly-Tyer's Carry-All, a small family business which manufactures the Folstaf and other products for fly fishing.*

New York City Harbor
New York
Joan Stoliar

*F*renetic by day, New York harbor is a quiet fantasy at night. For as far as you can see, the city's bridges are festooned with necklaces of light, like dew on spider webs. Beneath you, the harbor water is swift and black reflecting and mixing city lights. It's a magical setting. Reality swiftly reasserts itself, however, with the hit of a striper in the swirling current. Often running 20 -30", these babies furnish a level of excitement that's hard to beat, even in the Big Apple.

If you're coming to New York City on business, consider ending your workday with a few hours of convenient fishing. With pick-ups at 23rd St. and the World Financial Center at North Cove Yacht Harbor, you can be on the water and hooked up half an hour after you leave the office. It's possible to fish from the shore, but I don't advise it. I recommend exploring the harbor in a guide boat. A quality guide will have you casting to the edges of light from Governor's Island and the Statue of Liberty to the docks and coves of the East River.

We usually fish the harbor from sunset to about 11 PM. Our best fly fishing has been on an outgoing tide, before or after a new or full moon. New York Harbor is most productive when the water temperature is above 39° and when tides run higher and faster. While one can fish year-round, and enjoy it in the dead of winter, we usually fish spring and fall.

You are likely to be fishing Harbor waters 10 - 20' deep. The keys are a moderate cast (there is no call for tournament casting here) and staying alert while the line sinks. About 90% of your hits will probably occur at depths of 12 - 20' as the line sinks. When you feel your fly hit bottom, give it a little skip, let it sit, then another little hop. After this drop will be your next "hot moment." Then begin your retrieve using a slow, slow strip.

Types of Fish
Striped bass all year, bluefish from June to November.

Known Hatches or Baitfish
Moss bunker in summer. Silversides fall and winter. Cinder worms "hatch" in June (not hatching, just coming out to mate in large numbers).

Equipment to Use
Rods: 9 to 10', 8 weight, travel rod. Easier to get in taxi, bus or subway.
Reels: Any saltwater reel with a good drag.
Lines: The equivalent of a Teeny 250 or 300 line.
Leaders: 12 to 15 pound straight monofilament.
Wading or Boating: No wading. A guide with boat is my choice, though people do fish bulkheads.

Flies to Use
Streamers or poppers: Clouser Minnow & Lefty Deceiver, mostly white. Other colors can be added, blue and green particularly. Mylar good for imitating silversides. Popper useful in the fall.

When to Fish
March to June and mid-Oct. to January, nighttime on outgoing tide, a few days either side of a new or full moon when the tides run higher and faster.

Season & Limits
Catch and release year-round. You may keep one fish per day, 28" or better. We prefer to love 'em and leave 'em!

Accommodations & Services
Everything you will ever need is available in the New York area. Guides, and helpful fly and tackle shops are listed in the appendix.

Nearby Fly Fishing
An hour north, in the Croton Watershed, and west in New Jersey, there is good trout fishing. Within two hours, traveling north or northwest, you will find classic rivers and streams in the Catskills and Connecticut. Go east two hours to Long Island for salt and freshwater fishing.

Rating
A truly unique angling experience. On the right tides a definite 9 or 10.

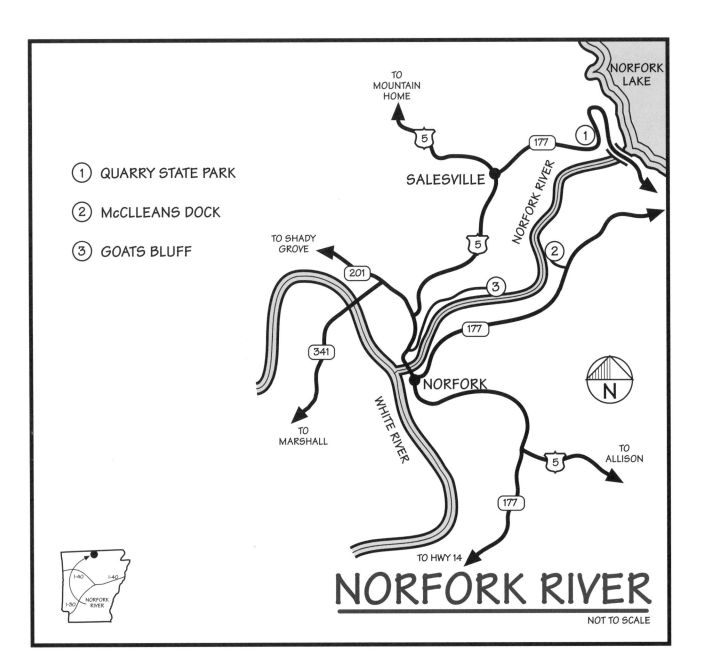

① QUARRY STATE PARK

② McCLLEANS DOCK

③ GOATS BLUFF

NORFORK LAKE

TO MOUNTAIN HOME

SALESVILLE

NORFORK RIVER

TO SHADY GROVE

TO MARSHALL

WHITE RIVER

NORFORK

TO ALLISON

TO HWY 14

NORFORK RIVER

NOT TO SCALE

Sister Carol Anne Corley was born in St. Louis to a sportsman father and artist mother. She grew up with a love of nature and outdoor activities, including fishing. In 1987, she bought a cheap fly outfit, taught herself to fly fish, and soon progressed to tying her own flies. To this day, she enjoys tying but loves teaching it even more, particularly to youth groups. Sister Carol Anne believes fly fishing and tying are ways to experience the beauty of God's creations and to enjoy, even celebrate, the wonders of His magnificent gifts to us. She maintains that "You can't fly fish in an ugly place or with an ugly spirit."

Norfork River
Arkansas
Sister Carol Anne Corley

While every serious fly angler has heard of Arkansas' White River, to the southeast of Mountain Home is a much shorter and lesser known cold water fishery, the Norfork River. With its four public access points, relatively easy wading, and beautiful scenery, this little river is my favorite fly fishing destination, especially the upper end of the river at Quarry State Park.

The boat ramp area at the State Park is the easiest access if you want to wade the upper Norfork. I have never drifted the river but have seen boats at the ramp with full limits. Directly in front of the boat ramps is a deep cut where drifting scuds, soft hackles, nymphs, and sow bugs under a strike indicator is your best bet. Don't underestimate this area . . . it can hold some large fish! Mid-stream below this cut, you'll find the first riffle, which covers a wide area with deeper cuts on both sides. Again, dead drifting small nymphs and stripping streamers can be very effective.

The wadeable water widens on the near side of the river as you move downstream. Stripping streamer patterns from deeper to shallower water can produce strikes. Be sure to let your fly drop deeply before beginning your retrieve. Dead drifting nymphs under a strike indicator will also work in this slower flow, but you must maintain a drag free drift to be effective. This section of the Norfolk can also provide wonderful dry fly opportunities during midge hatches that occur throughout the year.

The Norfolk's second riffle is a relatively small area with moss covered rocks and thin water. The fish are very spooky here and very selective. Down-size your tippet and your fly. As this water tails-out, it deepens considerably and flows under a large fallen tree. Deep pockets on both sides of this tree should be fished seriously. Big fish can hold in here.

If you're driving to the Norfork River from Mountain Home, follow Arkansas Highway 5 south to Salesville. Then take Highway 177 at Salesville and drive about two miles to Quarry State Park. This area contains the National Trout Hatchery, Dry Run Creek, and a handicapped access as well as camp grounds and boat ramps. This is an ideal place for a family vacation.

Type of Fish
Rainbows, browns, brookies, cutthroat, and what will appear to be cuttbows. They are not a true 50-50, hybrid mix.

Known Hatches
Midges hatch year-around. Mayfly hatches occur in the warm weather of early spring to mid-summer. Early spring and fall caddis hatches.

Equipment to Use
Rods: 9 foot, 5 or 6 weight.
Reels: Click or disc to match rod.
Lines: Weight forward floating.
Leaders: 7 - 9 foot, 4 to 6X.
Wading or Boating: Neoprene or breathable waders and felt soled boots. Drift fishing with local guides.

Flies to Use
Dries: Light Cahill, Adams, sulfur dun, Renegade, Elk Hair Caddis #14-18. Midge #16-20, Griffith's Gnat #18-22.
Nymphs: Red Ass, Partridge and Orange, Soft Hackle, Sow Bug #12-16, scud #12-18, Hare's Ear, Fox Squirrel #12-16.

Streamers: Wooly Buggers #8-12, Clouser Minnows #4-8. Other shad and sculpin patterns, San Juan Worm.

When to Fish
All year. Late summer can get hot particularly in August, and the late winter can be cold, particularly in February - March. Arkansas weather is very unpredictable, check the forecast.

Season & Limits
Fish year-round. Six fish per day limit. Only two, 16"+ brown, brook, cutthroat per day. No size limit on rainbows or cuttbows. The possession limit is twice the daily limit.

Accommodations & Services
Many hotels and all services in Mountain Home and Norfork (see appendix).

Rating
Good access, wading, and beauty, this is an overlooked favorite. For Arkansas, a 9.

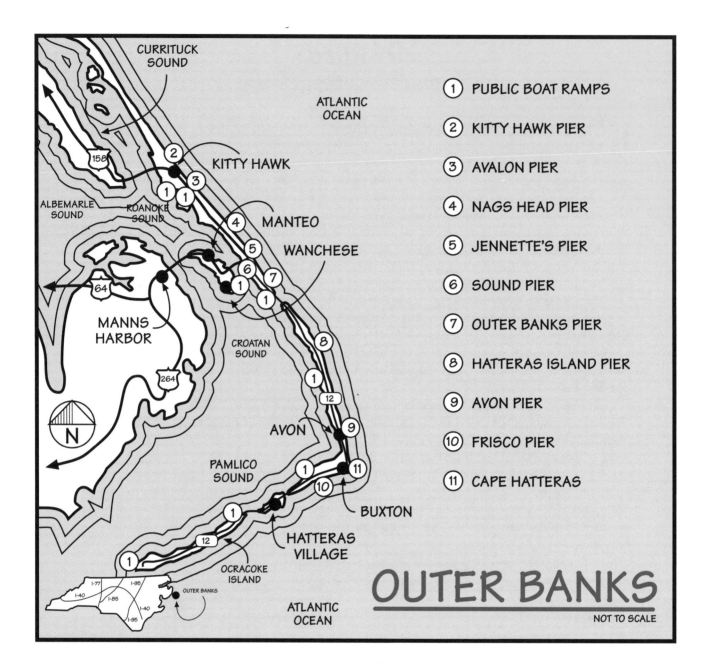

OUTER BANKS

NOT TO SCALE

① PUBLIC BOAT RAMPS

② KITTY HAWK PIER

③ AVALON PIER

④ NAGS HEAD PIER

⑤ JENNETTE'S PIER

⑥ SOUND PIER

⑦ OUTER BANKS PIER

⑧ HATTERAS ISLAND PIER

⑨ AVON PIER

⑩ FRISCO PIER

⑪ CAPE HATTERAS

Sarah Gardner is captain of an eighteen-foot, center-console, Parker charter boat specializing in fly and light tackle fishing trips. Angling has been her passion since childhood, and Sarah succumbed to the addiction of fly fishing ten years ago. Over the last five years, she has made most of her income from teaching, guiding and writing, all with a fly fishing focus. Her photographs, articles, and columns have appeared in regional as well as national magazines, and she also promotes fly fishing by giving slide shows and clinics throughout the eastern United States. Captain Sarah Gardner currently holds two IGFA woman's tippet records for bluefish.

The Outer Banks
North Carolina
Captain Sarah Gardner

Coastal North Carolina offers the best saltwater fly fishing north of the Florida Keys. A string of barrier islands, the Outer Banks's unique geography contributes to the diversity of the fish life found here. Anglers can cast flies to redfish in 2' of water or to white marlin in 200 fathoms.

The sounds between the Outer Banks and the mainland are loaded with fly rod quarry. Speckled trout and stripers are most common, but puppy drum can also be a challenge. When wading in the sound, stay near marsh edges and cast into deeper channels that hold fish. In late summer, near-shore wrecks attract hordes of bait and fly-munching predators. Anglers can tangle with a 10 lb. false albacore or a 60 lb. amberjack. In late fall, migrating stripers and blues arrive off the coast and stay for much of the winter.

There is plenty of public beach access on the Outer Banks. A favorite wading spot is behind the Coast Guard Station at Oregon Inlet or at Propeller Sloughs. Also try wading at Bode Island Lighthouse. There is nothing like releasing a speckled trout beneath the shadow of this classic old light. Anglers can also fish the entire length of the Outer Banks on the ocean side, but Oregon Inlet, Hatteras Light House, and Hatteras Inlet are better spots.

Fishing opportunities are diverse on the Outer Banks as are tackle needs. When wading in the sound use 7 or 8 weights as most fish are less than 5 pounds. When fishing the coast (on foot or by boat) move up in rod size. In the fall especially, many fish are over 5 pounds and looking for larger flies. A 9 or 10 weight rod works best as it does in the breaking surf and ocean currents.

The island's tackle shops, guides and hotels know the value of the internet. The Outer Banks may seem physically remote, but the fly fishing trip of a lifetime is only a mouse-click away.

Types of Fish
Sound: Speckled trout, gray trout, puppy (red) drum, small bluefish, stripers under 30".
Inshore: Amberjack, false albacore, Spanish mackerel, king mackerel, large stripers, bluefish.
Offshore: Blue & white marlin, yellow & blue fin tuna, dolphin, the easiest blue-water species to catch on a fly.

Known Baitfish
Sounds: Silver sides, bay anchovies, killy fish predominant.
Deeper water: Around wrecks, countless baitfish, 6" cigar minnow most common. In the fall, larger baitfish including bunker, croaker, gray trout (the major prey of stripers and blues) migrate along the coast.

Equipment to Use
Rods: 9 - 10", 7 to 10 weight depending on where you fish.
Reels: Disc drag, saltwater reels with good backing capacity.
Lines: Weight forward intermediate and fast sink.
Leaders: 71/2 foot, 0 to 3X.
Wading: Stripping basket, waders and boots.

Flies to Use
Black/red or orange, olive/tan, or chartreuse/white Clouser #2-5/0. When flies need to be large and able to sink, use Deceiver tied with lead on the hook shank.

When to Fish
Fly fish year-round. Peak season April - December. September - October fishing is good, water warm for swimming. Legendary bluefish and striper blitzes usually happen between Thanksgiving and Christmas.

Seasons & Limits
Seasons and limits change every year, sometimes in mid-season. Local tackle shops have regulations and tide sheets. As of this writing, fresh or saltwater license not needed. Catch & release always works best!

Accommodations & Services
Range is from primitive camping to expensive resorts. Hundreds of restaurants, many open early for anglers. Surf the net for more information.

Nearby Fly Fishing
Fresh and brackish water of Currituck Sound, northern end of the Outer Banks, excellent for pan fish, largemouth bass. A few fresh water ponds on the banks hold the same critters.

Rating
An excellent spot for fly anglers of all skills, tastes, and budgets, the Outer Banks deserves a 9.

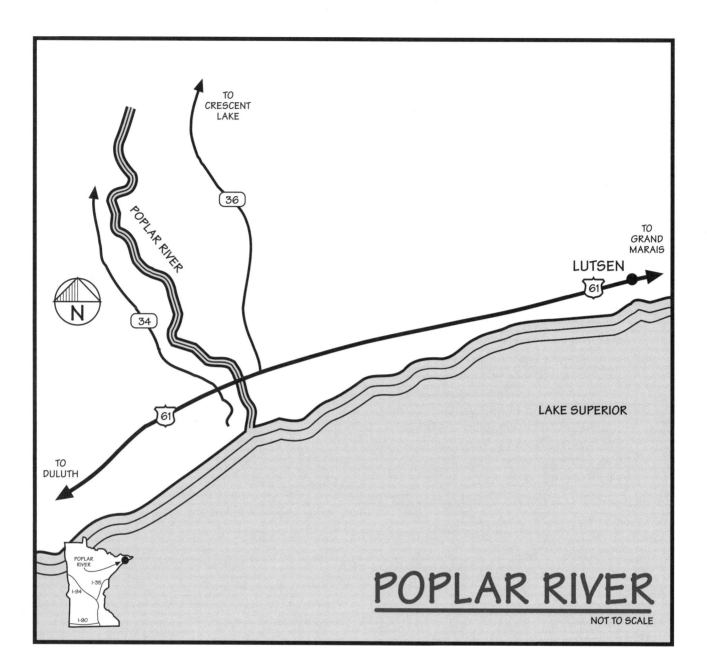

TO
CRESCENT
LAKE

36

POPLAR RIVER

TO
GRAND
MARAIS

LUTSEN

61

34

N

61

TO
DULUTH

LAKE SUPERIOR

POPLAR
RIVER

I-35

I-94

I-90

POPLAR RIVER

NOT TO SCALE

Nancy Jobe began fly fishing nine years ago and has since become a Federation of Fly Fishers Certified Casting Instructor. She helped found The Minnesota Women's Fly Fishing Club, and is a board member of the International Festival of Women Fly Fishers. Nancy and her family live near Minneapolis. She is finishing a book on fishing, My Angels Have Fins.

Poplar River
Minnesota
Nancy Willette Jobe

Located on the north shore of Lake Superior near Lutsen, Minnesota, the Poplar River occupies a special place in my heart because it was there, on Memorial Day, that my casting stroke came together, and I finally learned how to cast a fly rod. The rod became so fluid and powerfully hypnotic I never wanted to let go, and over fifty fishing trips later, the Poplar River remains one of my favorite fishing retreats.

The Poplar River meanders through several miles of northern Minnesota cedar and pine covered hills. During the spawning seasons, upstream pools are the most productive, but hiking down to the "pool" area can be a bit tricky, so be careful. My favorite fishing hole is where the river flows into Lake Superior. One early June evening several years ago, I landed an Atlantic salmon, a small steelhead, a lake trout, and a brook trout, all in only three hours!

Due to the variety of fish in the Poplar River, several fly fishing techniques can be used successfully, but nymphing with a streamer will produce results with any species. I find "high sticking" with three-or-four strike indicators spaced four inches apart near the end of the fly line produces the best drift. Often, any change in the alignment or sudden movement of these indicators means a fish has your fly! Use enough split shot to compensate for the varying depth and speed of the water, and keep slack out of your line. "Takes" are often hard to detect, especially when fishing for steelhead.

To reach the Poplar River, drive four hours northeast out of Minneapolis/St. Paul on Interstate 35 and Minnesota Highway 61. Entering Lutsen, you will notice the Lutsen Resort on the lake side of the highway. Turn right here and head down the hill to fish where the river enters the lake, or turn left for the upstream water. Parking and fishing at the resort are permitted.

Returning to the Poplar River is like coming home to me. It is comforting to find the fishing as good now as it was eleven years ago . . . a living testament to the practice of catch and release!

Types of Fish
Rainbows, Kamloops, lake trout, and brookies as well as coho, chinook, and pink salmon and even a few largemouth bass, walleye, and suckers (yuk!).

Equipment to Use
Rods: 9 foot, 6 to 8 weight.
Reels: Click or disc to match rod.
Lines: Double taper or weight forward floating or sink tip.
Leaders: 7 to 10 foot, 0 to 7X, depending on species.
Wading: Chest high waders and boots, upstream float tube fishing optional.

Flies to Use
Dries: Caddis, trico, hex, and PMD.
Nymphs: Serendipity, Hare's Ear, Prince, #14-20.
Streamers: Olive, brown, black Wooly Bugger, egg-sucking leach #8-12, chartreuse, yellow, fuchsia egg pattern.

When to Fish
April to June 15th for steelhead and the occasional salmon during their spawning run. All summer long for Kamloops, rainbows, and brookies. September 1st to November 1st for the fall salmon run.

Seasons & Limits
Limits vary by year and species. Please check with the local Department of Natural Resources before you fish. Better yet, practice catch & release, and you don't have to worry.

Accommodations & Services
The Lutsen Resort rents lodge rooms, villas, and cabins by the night or week. Other area resorts and hotels, The Village Inn, Mountain Inn, Bluefin Bay Resort, Holiday Inn Express, and others.

Rating
A sentimental favorite, a great fishery, a strong 9 or 10.

NOTE: GRAVEL ROAD CAN BE IMPASSABLE WHEN RAINING OR WET

SPORTSMAN'S INN, RIZUTO'S FLY SHOP

DURANGLERS FLY SHOP

AIRSTRIP

SAN JUAN RIVER

TO IGNACIO

511

CHURCH

511

539

TO HIGHWAY 64

173

TO AZTEC

ABE'S

TO BLOOMFIELD

① FEE PARKING, BRING A FEW BUCKS

② CABLE; CATCH & RELEASE UPSTREAM

③ FEE PARKING, TRAIL TO UPPER FLATS

④ UPPER FLATS

⑤ TEXAS HOLE

⑥ BAETIS BEND

⑦ LOWER FLATS

⑧ SIMON CANYON

⑨ FEWER BUT BIGGER FISH POSSIBLE

⑩ BOUNDARY SPECIAL REGULATION WATER

⑪ COTTONWOOD C.G.

⑫ TEXAS HOLE

N

SAN JUAN RIVER

NOT TO SCALE

SAN JUAN RIVER

I-25

I-40

I-40

I-10

I-25

Jan Crawford has been fly angling for over thirty-five years, fishing waters all over the United States and Canada as well as Mexico, Belize, New Zealand and Patagonia. In 1988, she retired after over twenty years in the computer industry to buy and operate the High Desert Angler, Santa Fe's premier fly fishing shop and guide service. Jan is a Federation Of Fly Fishers Certified Casting Instructor and has taught women-only fly fishing and tying classes for the past eight years, including seminars for Becoming an Outdoor Woman. She is currently on the board of directors of the International Women Fly fishers and a contributing author of two books, Fly Fishing in Northern New Mexico *and* Fly Patterns of Northern New Mexico.

San Juan River
New Mexico
Jan Crawford

*N*ew Mexico is blessed with hundreds of mountain streams, tailwaters and trophy trout lakes, but, if you're looking for large trout, the San Juan River is by far the best known and most exciting of these waters. The state's consistently sunny southwestern climate generally allows quality days, even in the dead of winter. Visitors from around the world come to enjoy year-round fly fishing for 16 to 20", well-fed rainbows as well as a sprinkling of browns and cutthroat.

The San Juan has 8 miles of public access to easily wadeable water, yet is large enough to fish by drift boat. The upper half of this excellent water is managed as a trophy fishery. Anglers often catch several trout over 20" in a day, and nearly all of them are released.

The main fish foods on the San Juan are midges and aquatic worms, plus three major cycles of blue winged olives each year. A pale morning dun hatch of varying heaviness happens in late July through late August. After a June or July rain, sporadic falls of large carpenter ants make for glorious dry fly fishing. Some years also bring a good caddis hatch in June. Egg patterns in winter and San Juan Worms and leech patterns all year give anglers a fall back tactic if no hatches are occurring. Of course, San Juan trout are always feeding on midges, subsurface if not on top.

Most successful San Juan anglers use three-to-five weight rods. Longer rods assist better line control for drag free drifts in sometimes difficult currents. 6X tippets are standard, though special conditions may allow 5X or demand 7X. These fish are not angler or line shy but are very picky about patterns and proper drift.

The San Juan River is 3 hours by car from the Albuquerque airport and 1 hour from Durango, Colorado. Pueblo ruins, hiking, and local arts and crafts provide entertainment for non-anglers.

Type of Fish
Rrainbows, browns cutthroat and carp.

Known Hatches
Blue winged olives #18-22, pale morning duns #14-16, carpenter ants #12, midges #18-24 caddis #14-16, aquatic worms, and leeches.

Equipment to Use
Rods: 8 foot or longer, 3-6 weight.
Reels: Smooth drag (click or disc).
Lines: Weight forward or double taper floating.
Leaders: 7 to 9 foot, 5 or 6X.
Wading & Boating: Felt or studded felt soled boots and warm chest waders. Dories when river above 400 cfs.

Flies to Use
Dries: Parachute, standard Adams, blue winged olive dun, Chocolate Emerger, Griffith's Gnat, trico Hairwing Dun, black and BWO Brooks Sprouts.
Nymphs: San Juan Worm, annelid, subsurface midge pattern. Fly shops in Santa Fe, Albuquerque and on the river have the latest "midge de jour."
Streamers: Black and gray leech pattern.

When to Fish
All year. Wading difficult April - May with high flows over 1500 cfs. Less crowded in fall, winter, spring, and midweek.

Seasons & Limits
Fish all year. First mile below dam is no kill. Next 3 miles, 1 fish over 20". Rest of river, 5 fish daily. Upper waters single, barbless artificials only. One and 5 day licenses available.

Accommodations & Services
Campgrounds, lodges and motels and one restaurant/bar along the river. Camping at Navajo Lake. Complete services in Aztec (20 miles away) and Farmington. Guide services for lake and river fishing readily available.

Nearby Fly Fishing
Navajo Lake for small and largemouth bass, pike, carp, trout, and salmon.

Rating
Not a river of solitude but of lots of big fish. A top trout stream in the world, and a solid 10 if you don't mind fishing in sight of a dozen other anglers.

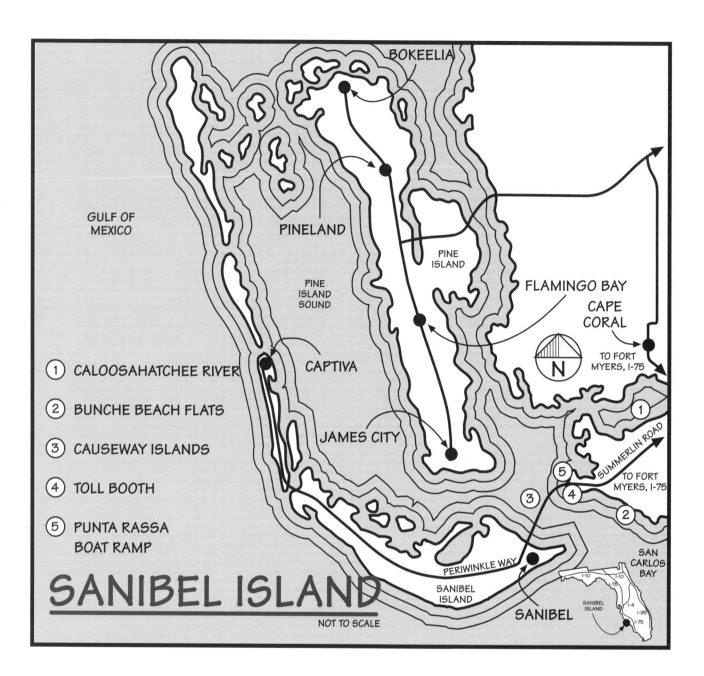

GULF OF
MEXICO

BOKEELIA

PINELAND

PINE
ISLAND

PINE
ISLAND
SOUND

FLAMINGO BAY

CAPE
CORAL

N

TO FORT
MYERS, I-75

① CALOOSAHATCHEE RIVER

CAPTIVA

② BUNCHE BEACH FLATS

③ CAUSEWAY ISLANDS

JAMES CITY

①

SUMMERLIN ROAD

TO FORT
MYERS, I-75

④ TOLL BOOTH

⑤

④

⑤ PUNTA RASSA
BOAT RAMP

③

②

SANIBEL ISLAND

NOT TO SCALE

PERIWINKLE WAY

SANIBEL
ISLAND

SAN
CARLOS
BAY

SANIBEL

SANIBEL
ISLAND

Mina Hemingway, granddaughter of Ernest Hemingway, caught her first sailfish at the age of nine and has been fly fishing for twenty-five years. The former owner of the Austin Angler Fly Shop where she hosted fly fishing charters around the world, Mina now spends her time promoting woman's fishing tournaments and speaking at Ladies Let's Go Fishing seminars in Florida. She is on the board of the Ostego Bay Marine Science Center and the Sanibel Island Tarpon Hunters Club. As a member of the International Game Fish Association, Mina and her husband, Jon Rothenberg, work in conjunction with Hemingway Kids, Inc. and the I.G.F.A. to promote Junior Angler tournaments.

Sanibel Island
Florida
Mina Hemingway and Carlene F. Brennen

On March 22, 1885 in Tarpon Bay off Sanibel Island, W.H. Wood of New York City, fishing with local guide John Smith, landed the first tarpon ever taken on rod and reel. Wood, himself, reported in the April 23, 1885 issue of *Forest & Stream* that his fish was 5', 9" long and weighed 93 pounds. He fought the tarpon for slightly more than 26 minutes. A story about Wood's feat in the *London Observer* praised what was already being called the greatest game fish in the sport, concluding that "Sportsmen may yet go to Florida for the tarpon, as they go to the Arctic Zone for reindeer, walrus and musk-oxen." Since Wood's historic catch, Sanibel Island has become famous for its large runs of tarpon. There are stories of anglers spotting schools of tarpon 8 miles across in 40' of water. On a one-day trip, three anglers jumped 27 tarpon, catching and releasing 7. And then there was the two-day fishing rodeo where 60 boats caught and released no fewer than 300 tarpon. To this day, the pristine, historic area around Sanibel Island retains its reputation as one of the West Coast of Florida's prime tarpon hunting grounds.

During April, May and June, the concentration of tarpon around Sanibel Island is one of the highest in the world. Here, large schools of silver kings stop their northern migration to feed on almost endless schools of mullet, shad, catfish, and Spanish mackerel. In these months, a combination of calm water (typically seas of 2' or less) and good visibility create ideal conditions for poling and casting to large pods of tarpon. Truly, this is offshore fly fishing at its very best.

The best way to fish for these wonderful creatures is to cruise slowly along the beaches until you find a pod of rolling tarpon. While drifting, you cast to moving or daisy-chaining pods, either to the outside or lead fish, depending on your casting angle. Never cast to the middle of a pod as you might spook the fish. As an added bonus, schools of permit numbering up to 500 or more may accompany the pods of tarpon you are casting to. It's not a bad idea to have a Del Brown's Permit Fly rigged up.

To reach Sanibel Island, take Exit #21 off I-75 out of Fort Myers, Florida. Go west on Daniels Road across US41 where Daniels turns into Cypress Lake Drive. At Summerlin Road turn left and continue to the Sanibel Causeway. The Punta Rassa public boat ramp is on the right before entering the tollbooth. A hundred years ago, Punta Rassa was once known internationally for its Tarpon House where the likes of Frederic Remington and Thomas Edison once stayed and fished for tarpon, sharks, saw fish and giant rays (then called devil fish). A public boat ramp on Sanibel Island is on the immediate left after exiting the causeway. Straight ahead, at a four-way stop turn left on Periwinkle Way to reach Old Town Sanibel at the eastern end of the island. Here, you will find a full-service marina, restaurants, shopping, and other accommodations as well as an historic lighthouse, fishing pier, and beaches. Turn right on Periwinkle Way for a full-service fly shop.

Fly fishing for tarpon and permit off the beaches of Sanibel Island has been one of Florida's best kept secrets. Mina's grandfather, Nobel laureate and avid outdoorsman Ernest Hemingway, enjoyed the thrill of fishing for big tarpon before he ever set a hook in a sailfish or marlin. Papa never fished the waters around Sanibel Island, but his father, grandfather, and sister, Carol, did. You should too!

(Continued next page)

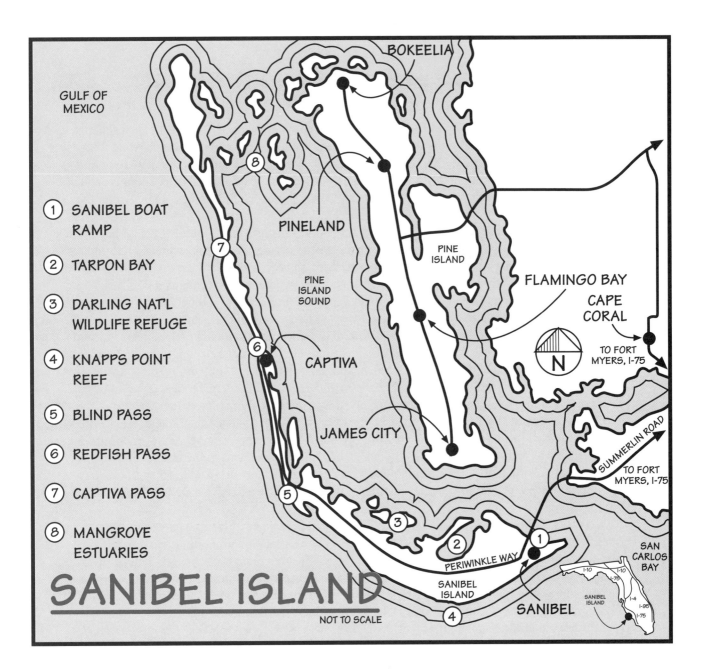

GULF OF
MEXICO

① SANIBEL BOAT
   RAMP

② TARPON BAY

③ DARLING NAT'L
   WILDLIFE REFUGE

④ KNAPPS POINT
   REEF

⑤ BLIND PASS

⑥ REDFISH PASS

⑦ CAPTIVA PASS

⑧ MANGROVE
   ESTUARIES

BOKEELIA

PINELAND

PINE
ISLAND

PINE
ISLAND
SOUND

CAPTIVA

JAMES CITY

FLAMINGO BAY
CAPE
CORAL

N

TO FORT
MYERS, I-75

SUMMERLIN ROAD

TO FORT
MYERS, I-75

SAN
CARLOS
BAY

PERIWINKLE WAY

SANIBEL
ISLAND

SANIBEL

SANIBEL ISLAND

NOT TO SCALE

Carlene F. Brennen is a publisher and wildlife portrait photographer living on Sanibel Island Florida. Founder and first president of the Sanibel Island Tarpon Hunters Club, she was the first woman president of both the Fort Myers Beach Tarpon Hunters Club and the Sanibel Island Fishing Club. Carlene and author Randy Wayne White co-published Tarpon Tales, Lost Stories and Research. *She writes a weekly fishing column for the* Sanibel-Captiva Shopper's Guide *and is currently working on a book about women who fish for tarpon. Carlene and her husband, Terry Brennen, co-own Brennen's Tarpon Tale Inn Bed and Breakfast on Sanibel Island.*

Types of Fish
Tarpon, sharks, permit, redfish, and snook.

Known Baitfish
Glass minnow, thread-fin herring, pilchard, Spanish sardine.

Equipment to Use
Rods: 9 foot, 9 to 12 weight.
Reels: Saltwater disc drag, 300 yds. 20 - 30 lb. backing.
Lines: Weight forward, mono-core, med. sink to match rod.
Leaders: Tapered 60-50-40 lb. butt section looped to 16 or 20 lb. class tippet, 80 lb. shock tippet with Huffnagle Knot.
Boating: Tarpon can only be caught from skiffs.

Flies to Use
Natural baitfish color Deceivers, tarpon flies in orange, black, purple, red/white, pink/white. Epoxy head Deceivers in natural baitfish colors similar to thread fin herring. Wing is white bucktail topped by olive bucktail, peacock herl.

When to Fish
April, May, June are prime, but Tarpon are around March - October. Some resident tarpon that can be found in the back bays and rivers all year. Local guide, Captain Rick Featherstone, has fly fished this area for 20 years. He says tarpon are low light feeders; best to fish the first 2 hours after sunrise or the last 2 hours before sunset. Cast with the rising or setting sun to your back. In the morning, start along the beaches in 10' of water and work your way out into the deeper waters of the Gulf of Mexico.

Seasons & Limits
The season is year-round with a two fish limit per day. To harvest and possess a tarpon, you must have a $50 tarpon kill tag for each fish, payable in advance. Isn't it easier and better to just release them?

Accommodations & Services
Brennen's Tarpon Tale Inn Bed & Breakfast, five upscale bungalows nestled in a tropical garden atmosphere. The inn has parking for boats, trailers, and RV's and is within easy walking distance to restaurants, deli, grocery store, and shops. Sanibel Marina and Boat House Rentals, the island's only full-service marina, is just down the street. A fly shop, campground, and the J. N. Ding Darling National Wildlife Refuge are nearby. Brennen's Tarpon Tale Inn Bed & Breakfast, 941-472-0932.
Magic Hook Charters, 941-455-0006.
Sanibel Marina, 941-472-2723.

Nearby Fly Fishing
Nearby mangrove-lined estuaries offer some of Florida's best red fish, spotted sea trout, and snook fishing. This can be excellent shallow water, sight fishing accessed by wading out of a boat or from shore.

Rating
Tarpon found in abundance in April, May, and June and snook, redfish, and spotted sea trout plentiful throughout the year. Without a doubt, we rate Sanibel Island a 10.

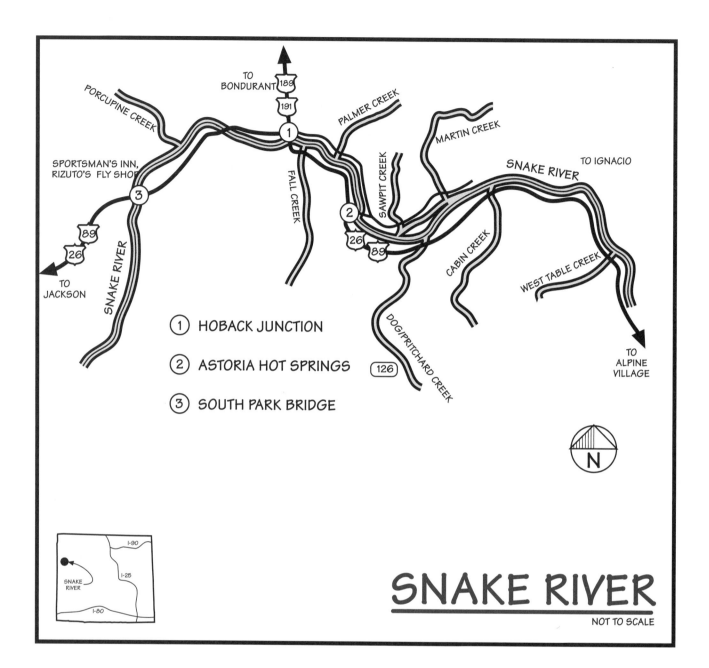

1 HOBACK JUNCTION

2 ASTORIA HOT SPRINGS

3 SOUTH PARK BRIDGE

SNAKE RIVER

NOT TO SCALE

Lori-Ann Murphy has many years of experience as a professional fly fishing guide on her favorite rivers in Idaho, Wyoming, and Montana. Her lifelong passion for fly fishing has been extremely contagious. Lori-Ann is an advisor to The Orvis Company, and she can be found in the off-season giving fly fishing presentations at sport shows and banquets. Lori-Ann is the owner/operator of Reel Women Fly Fishing Outfitters based just over the hill from Jackson Hole, Wyoming in Victor, Idaho. The Reel Women Guide team offer fresh and saltwater schools, professional guiding for all anglers, women's guide schools, and women's destination fishing trips.

Snake River
Wyoming
Lori-Ann Murphy

Centuries ago, the Snake River held treasures for fur trappers as well as the Native American tribes that lived along its banks. There is actually an American Indian hand-sign that means "Snake River." Today, the river still holds treasure. It will make you laugh with every cast as you watch another eager cutthroat eat your fly. The Snake is one of those "feel good" fishin' rivers.

The Snake River in Wyoming is one of the last strongholds for the Fine Spotted Snake River Cutthroat. Although the locals have their secret spots and techniques, this is not a "big fish" river, but its accommodating trout loves to rise to the dry fly. With the river's multiple mayfly and stonefly hatches, a well-presented dry fly is a sure bet to fool a fish.

The best way to fish the Snake is from a drift boat, stopping along the way to wade side channels and gravel bars. The Snake is often difficult to wade due to fast, strong currents and slick boulders on the bottom. The secret of this river is not to wade out too far—fish are sometimes in water that is ankle deep. Select a piece of water like a shallow "pour" over a gravel bar, watch it, and soon you'll see evidence of Mr. Fine Spotted Snake River Cutthroat.

You can try to match the Snake River's hatches of pale morning duns, blue winged olives, or golden stones, or you can just throw a #12 Royal Wulff all day and have a blast. The Humpy, developed right here in Jackson Hole, is another favorite pattern, and big hoppers are a must as fall approaches. Don't be afraid to go deep and heavy with streamers in slow moving pocket water. The river's "old timers" like to strip a Muddler Minnow or black Wooly Bugger slowly by the banks. The proper "twitch" can be deadly.

Spend a couple days checking out the different sections of the Snake from just below Jackson Lake Dam all the way to West Table. If you are floating, South Park to Pritchard or "Dog" Creek is straight forward while Pritchard to West Table has some tricky spots for rowing.

Types of Fish
Fine Spotted Snake River Cutthroat and Rocky Mountain Whitefish.

Known Hatches
PMD's, golden stones, BWO's, and terrestrials.

Equipment to Use
Rods: 9 foot, 4 to 6 weight, but lighter rods can be fun.
Reels: Click or disk to match rod.
Lines: Weight forward or double taper floating to match rod.
Leaders: 7 to 9 foot, 4 and 5X.
Wading or Boating: Felt soled boots (some people like cleats), chest waders with belt. Wet wade in summer. Drift boaters will encounter nothing greater than a Class II. There are some eddy lines to keep in mind as you look down river.

Flies to Use
Dries: PMD #14-18, Golden stonefly #12-14, BWO #16-20.
Dry Attractors: Stimulator, Royal Wulff, Humpy #12-16.
Nymphs: Beadhead and soft hackle Pheasant Tail #16-18.
Streamers: Tequeelie, Wooly Bugger, Muddler Minnow.

When to Fish
Late July through November 1st.

Seasons & Limits
Trout season opens April 1st. Depending on runoff, there is a week or two in April that can be fishable. The season closes November 1st.

Accommodations & Services
Reel Women Fly Fishing Outfitters (208-787-2657) for informative and enjoyable fly fishing outings. Jackson Hole offers an array of fly shops, B & B's, lodges, motels, hotels, and dude ranches as well as all other services (see appendix).

Nearby Fly Fishing
You are only a short drive from the fabled waters in Yellowstone Park and eastern Idaho.

Rating
A good day on the river is always a 10.

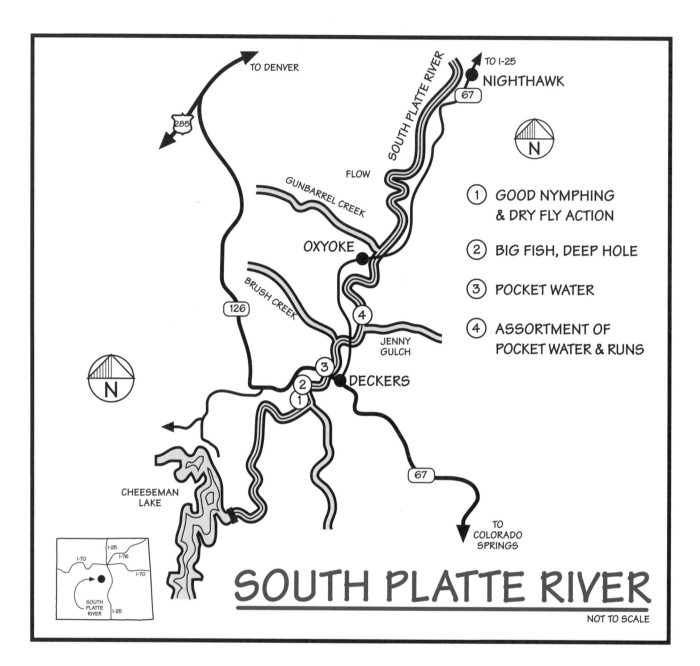

TO DENVER

TO I-25

NIGHTHAWK

67

SOUTH PLATTE RIVER

FLOW

GUNBARREL CREEK

285

OXYOKE

N

① GOOD NYMPHING & DRY FLY ACTION

② BIG FISH, DEEP HOLE

③ POCKET WATER

④ ASSORTMENT OF POCKET WATER & RUNS

BRUSH CREEK

126

④

JENNY GULCH

③

N

②

①

DECKERS

67

CHEESEMAN LAKE

TO COLORADO SPRINGS

SOUTH PLATTE RIVER

NOT TO SCALE

I-70 I-25 I-76 I-70 SOUTH PLATTE RIVER I-25

Dana Rikimaru is the Head Instructor of the Orvis Colorado Fly Fishing School as well as an Orvis Endorsed Guide and Federation of Fly Fishers Certified Casting Instructor. Dana works and guides for the Blue Quill Angler in Evergreen, Colorado. She is author of the book, Fly Fishing, A Woman's Guide.

South Platte River
Colorado
Dana Rikimaru

*L*ocated in the foothills of Colorado's Pike National Forest, Cheesman Canyon is breathtakingly beautiful. Ponderosa pine and Colorado blue spruce carpet the red rock landscape, sloping down to house-sized, granite boulders that line the South Platte River. This popular tailwater below Cheesman Reservoir is known for its spectacular surroundings and feisty trout.

Like most tailwaters, the South Platte is known for its prolific population of small flies, including a large population of Baetis and midges. Flies #18 - 24 are considered standard on this, oftentimes, very technical water. It's also a great river for sight fishing, often requiring precise, drag-free, dead drifts to well-educated trout.

Short-line nymphing techniques produce the most consistent fishing on this section of the South Platte. Small strike indicators are advised with yarn being the preferred material. There are times when you can be successful casting a dry fly, and this fishing will be more productive if you look for rising fish and then cast to an individual fish.

If you want to hike into Cheesman Canyon, you can access it either from the top by the reservoir or by taking the more popular route from downstream. Watch for the Wigwam Campground at the bottom of a steep grade on County Road 126. Park at the campground and access the trailhead by following a path that crosses over small Wigwam Creek. Follow the path uphill and, at the top, you will find a wooden plaque with a map detailing the three-mile trail into the canyon.

If hiking 3 miles to Gold Medal trout water is not your cup of tea, there's still a lot of great fishing downstream of Cheesman Canyon and below the private Wigwam Club. The Lone Rock Campground marks the first public access area below the canyon. From there and downstream of Deckers, the road is paved for approximately 8 miles. It then turns into a well-kept dirt road where parking is permitted only in designated areas.

Types of Fish
Rainbow, cuttbow and brown trout.

Known Hatches or Baitfish
Baetis (blue winged olives), tricos are the primary hatches. PMD's, caddis, stoneflies smaller, less prolific hatches.

Equipment to Use
Rods: 8 to 9 foot, 4 to 6 weight.
Reels: Click or disc of moderate weight.
Lines: Weight forward or double taper floating.
Leaders: 7 foot, 5 to 7X.
Wading: Walk and wade fishing. Felt soled wading boots, chest waders as water temperature ranges from 40-60º even in the middle of summer.

Flies to Use
Dries: Parachute or thorax BWO #20-24, spent-wing trico #22-24, Elk Hair Caddis #14-18, yellow Stimulator #16-18.
Nymphs: Pheasant Tail, Miracle Nymph #20-22, RS2 Emerger #20-24, San Juan Worm #14, scuds #14-18.
Streamers: Wooly Bugger #6-12, S. Platte Streamer #6-10, Muddler Minnow #6-12.

When to Fish
Wintertime, 9 a.m. - 3 p.m. Spring, summer, and fall, fish after the sun hits the water until it sets.

Seasons & Limits
Fish year-round. Cheesman Canyon, all catch & release, barbless artificials only. Lone Rock to Scraggy View, 2 fish over 16", artificial flies and lures only. Downstream of Scraggy View, limit 8 fish. Catch & release is not required on all sections of the river, but the practice is highly encouraged.

Accommodations & Services
Deckers, on the S. Platte, has fly shop (Flies & Lies 303- 647-2237), lodging, small country store. Streamside camping at Wigwam, Lone Rock. More camping downstream from Deckers. Next nearest services 30 min. drive north or south.

Nearby Fly Fishing
Lot of great fishing on other sections of the South Platte.

Rating
This area is a 7, both the canyon and downstream sections.

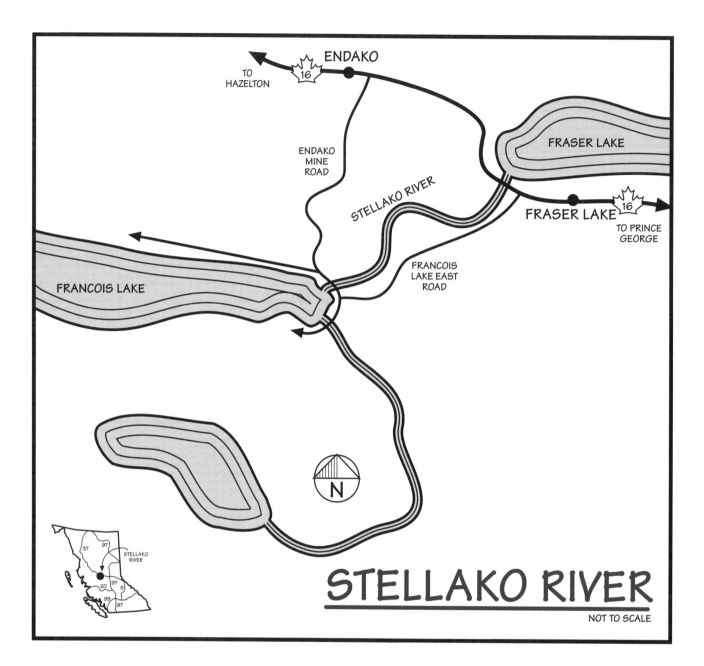

TO
HAZELTON

ENDAKO

16

ENDAKO
MINE
ROAD

FRASER LAKE

STELLAKO RIVER

FRASER LAKE

16

TO PRINCE
GEORGE

FRANCOIS
LAKE EAST
ROAD

FRANCOIS LAKE

N

STELLAKO RIVER

NOT TO SCALE

Mallory Burton lives on the Northeast coast of British Columbia where she works as a regional coordinator for special educational technology. During the fall and spring, she fishes for salmon and steelhead on the coast. She spends her summers fishing tiny dry flies in Alberta and Montana. Mallory has written for fly fishing trade magazines and anthologies for the past decade but swears that she'll never write a "how to/where to" piece. Reading the Water, *her first collection of fiction and humor, was published in 1995 by Keokee Press, A second edition is forthcoming.*

Stellako River
British Columbia, Canada
Mallory Burton

*I*f you've been skunked on the Henry's Fork and Silver Creek, you'll get skunked on the Stellako too. Especially if you leave before the wind quits, if you can't manage a drag-free float, if you can't fish by ear in the dark, or if you free-fall down the Goat Trail. If you do come, be prepared to pay your dues, because there are no guides, and it takes years to learn this river.

The Stellako River, which connects Francois Lake and Fraser Lake, is approximately 7 miles long with trail access for most of its length. Recent windstorms have created a great deal of "blow down" on some sections of the trail, but it is possible to wade around most of the bad trail sections. Keep an eye out for black bears.

The most sensible way to fish the Stellako is to sit on your cabin porch with a glass of good scotch until you actually see fish rising. Only then should you put on your waders. Spectacular hatches are usually evening affairs. Typically, the wind will build for three or four days and then suddenly stop. This is when you can expect the bugs to pop. If you insist on going out when there is no insect activity, cast ahead of and behind boulders, along rocky shelves, and under overhanging brush with a minnow or an attractor pattern.

Quartering upstream or across to rising fish does not work very well on drag-shy Stellako rainbows. Cast straight upstream and strip like mad or cast straight downstream and quickly feed out slack. Quartering downstream is also effective. Make a reach cast followed by a quick upstream mend to send the fly down ahead of your line.

The Stellako is located about 2 hours west of Prince George in northern British Columbia and is accessible by air from Vancouver. Heading west a few kilometers past the town of Fraser Lake, you'll come to a single flashing yellow traffic signal just before the highway crosses the Stellako River. Turn left and follow the road 11 kilometers to the Stellako River Lodge.

Types of Fish
"Hand-painted," darkly colored rainbows as well as suckers, whitefish, and a small fall run of sockeye.

Known Hatches & Baitfish
A few stoneflies during the day, cream and black-bodied mayflies, caddis, and, rarely, large gray mayflies and their spinners in the evening. Sculpins abound.

Equipment to Use
Rods: 9 foot, 4 to 6 weight, depending on the wind.
Reels: Click or disc to match rod.
Lines: Double taper or weight forward floating.
Leaders: Under 9 foot, 4 to 5X.
Wading & Boating: Neoprene waders and boots. Use a staff for high water, faster currents, or river crossing. Fishing from boats not permitted. Some use rafts or kickboats to drift. Check the condition of the falls first and portage them. A guided raft trip is a good way to scout the river.

Flies to Use
Dries: Royal Wulff, Stimulator, Sofa Pillow, gray drake, PMD, black gnat, Elk Hair Caddis, lime green Humpy.
Nymphs: Bead headed Hare's Ear and soft hackle.

Streamers: Muddler Minnow.
The lodge's hot flies sell out fast. Bring tying kit, and tie the patterns in their *empty* bins.

When to Fish
You can pick up a few fish during the day, but the best fishing is always in the early morning or evening.

Seasons & Limits
Open June 1st to November 14th, classified water. Upper section, fly fishing only with single, barbless hooks, no external lead or strike indicators.

Accommodations & Services
The Stellako Lodge, dining room with Swiss food, housekeeping cabins and camping hookups. Motel, restaurants, and groceries in the town of Fraser Lake. Several commercial campgrounds on nearby Francois Lake.

Nearby Fly Fishing
When the wind is too severe, use float tubes on nearby lakes.

Rating
A river for the experienced angler, I'd give it a 7.

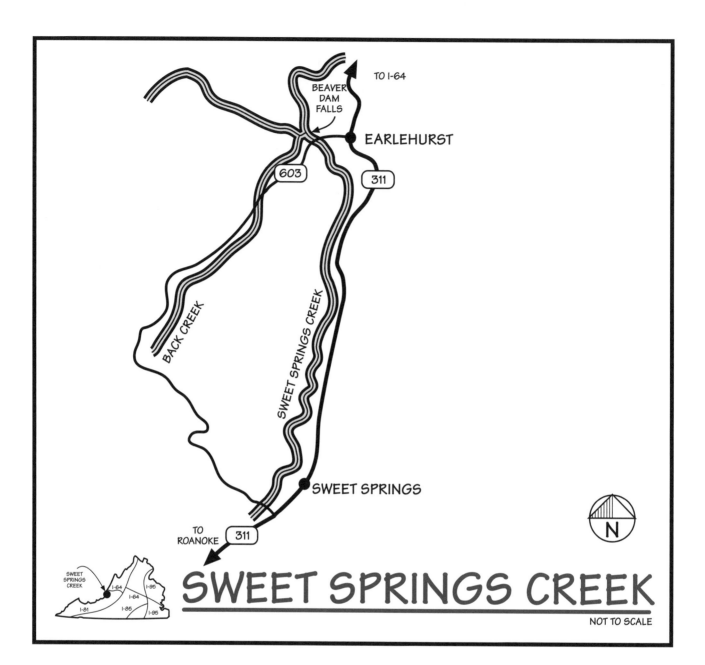

TO I-64

BEAVER DAM FALLS

EARLEHURST

603

311

BACK CREEK

SWEET SPRINGS CREEK

SWEET SPRINGS

TO ROANOKE   311

N

SWEET SPRINGS CREEK

SWEET SPRINGS CREEK

I-64   I-64
I-81   I-85   I-95

NOT TO SCALE

Rhea Topping has been a National Director for the Federation Of Fly Fishers since 1996. She is also an FFF Certified Master Casting Instructor and teaches for the Wulff School of Fly Fishing and Vermont's Becoming an Outdoor Woman Fly Fishing Program. Rhea serves on the Pro Staffs of Ross Reels, Simms, Scientific Angler, and G. Loomis and was the Associate Producer of Joan Wulff's successful new video, Dynamics of Fly Casting. *She lives near Middleburg, Virginia where she is working on a book about fly fishing etiquette when her duties as a real estate broker allow her time.*

Sweet Springs Creek
Virginia
Rhea R. Topping

Running through a remote valley in Allegheny County, Virginia, Sweet Springs Creek on Beaver Dam Falls Farm is unquestionably one of the most idyllic pieces of trout water I've had the privilege to fish. This water is a "knock your waders off" storybook setting!

Three miles downstream from its source, Sweet Springs Creek flows at the rate of 6,500 gallons per minute through the 250 acre, Beaver Dam Falls Farm. Owned by Kathleen and Barry Goodwin, this working farm has operated as a catch and release trout fishery since the mid-1990's.

The greatest challenge at Sweet Springs Creek lies not in hooking fish but trying not to get too distracted by the beauty of the place. Moss-and-fern-covered-limestone waterfalls split the water into the cleverly named Upper, Middle, and Lower sections.

The Upper section, which ribbons its way through a lush meadow, consists of a series of small pools and riffles. Often no more than a few feet across, this section truly challenges an angler's casting and stalking skills.

The shortest of the three, the Middle section is slightly wider than the Upper with pools and runs that are deceptively deep in spots. Here, the better fish are usually taken on nymphs.

The Lower section of the creek is the real scene-stealer! Because of accessibility and pressure, this section offers perhaps the ultimate challenge. Here, the creek gradually warms and widens into more of a freestone river. Large red cedars line the banks, and the woods are filled with black bear, deer, wild turkeys, and grouse.

Below the big falls, large, deep pools hold equally proportioned rainbow trout. Inaccessible to an angler on foot using normal trout gear, this water could be fished from a belly boat or with a spey rod, both of which I intend to try this spring.

Sweet Springs Creek is 55 miles from the Roanoke Airport, 26 miles from the Lewisburg Airport, and less than 4 hours by car from Washington, D.C.. Call 540-559-2622 or e-mail bgoodwin@cfw.com for specific directions. Be sure to tell them Rhea sent you.

Type of Fish
Rainbow trout, natural and stocked, up to 30".

Known Hatches & Baitfish
Winter: BWO's, midges, and early black stoneflies. *Spring:* Quill Gordons, BWO's, gray fox, march browns, midges. *Summer:* Sulfurs, green drakes, caddis, tricos, Cahills, and mahogany duns. *Fall:* October caddis, BWO's, tricos, midges, terrestrials. *All year:* sculpin, crawfish.

Equipment to Use
Rods: 8 to 9 foot, 1 to 6 weight. Spey rod for lower section.
Wading: Click or disc to match rod.
Lines: Weight forward floating or sink tip to match rod.
Leaders: 7 to 15 foot, 4 to 7X.
Wading: The creek is easily wadeable from either bank.

Flies to Use
Dries: Adams, Wulff, rusty spinner, Griffith's Gnat, Stimulator, Renegade, Chernobyl Ant.
Nymphs: Soft Hackle, CK Nymph, Hare's Ear, Prince, Zug Bug, and PT. Beadhead are very effective on all of the above.
Streamers: Dace & "Ghost" pattern, Wooly Bugger, Zonker, Bunny Leech, Muddler Minnow, Mickey Finn, Clouser, crawfish, San Juan Worm, Glo-Bug.

Season & Limits
Open all year, limit six rods, daily fee $45/rod. Multiple day rates, $40/day. Catch & release only.

Accommodations & Services
Old Earlehurst B&B, Milton Hall in Callahan, Greenbriar Hotel and Wylie House, in White Sulphur Springs. The Homestead in Hot Springs. Chain motels and all services in Covington and White Sulphur Springs.

Nearby Fly Fishing
Excellent fishing on Second Creek, the Greenbriar, Jackson, Cowpasture and Bullpasture rivers, Lake Moomaw.

Rating
Come see for yourself, an honest 10, and then some!

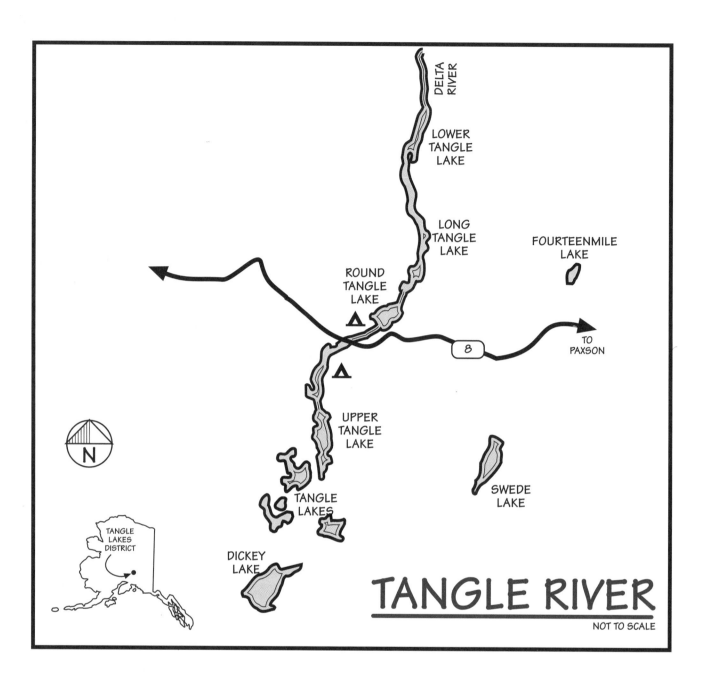

DELTA
RIVER

LOWER
TANGLE
LAKE

LONG
TANGLE
LAKE

FOURTEENMILE
LAKE

ROUND
TANGLE
LAKE

8

TO
PAXSON

UPPER
TANGLE
LAKE

SWEDE
LAKE

N

TANGLE
LAKES
DISTRICT

TANGLE
LAKES

DICKEY
LAKE

TANGLE RIVER

NOT TO SCALE

Cecilia "Pudge" Kleinkauf has been fly fishing for over fifteen years and has owned and operated Women's Flyfishing for nearly as long. She has lived in Alaska since 1969 and regularly ties flies and presents casting clinics and slide shows in Alaska and the lower forty-eight states. Pudge has been featured in numerous newspaper articles as well as on the Alaska affiliates of all three major television networks. She serves on the pro staff of Ross Reels, Mustad, and Patagonia and is currently the secretary of International Womens Fly Fishers.

Tangle River
Alaska
Cecilia "Pudge" Kleinkauf

*T*he 130-mile Denali Highway in the interior of Alaska passes through the famous Tangle River/Tangle Lakes District known as "grayling heaven." Despite their coppery, tannin color, the waters of the district provide perfect wading, canoeing, or float tubing water for the fly fisher as well as perfect habitat for the elegant arctic grayling. Splendid scenery, a profusion of wild-flowers and wildlife, and a fish whose proclivity to take a dry fly exceeds even that of the most eager trout, combine to make the Tangle River/Tangle Lakes region of Alaska my favorite water

These grayling will test your casting accuracy by holding tenaciously in narrow feeding lanes. They will also try your patience either by following your fly down their narrow feeding lane for some distance before taking or by rising gracefully up over your fly and taking it "on the down" as they re-enter the water. Inexperienced grayling anglers often miscalculate the hook set and come up empty handed. Also, in spite of their eagerness to take a dry fly, grayling can be quite leader shy, and a drag-free drift with the leader squarely behind the fly is generally essential to hooking them. You must mend both line and leader to insure the fish sees the fly first. Grayling can also put up quite a fight but tire quickly due to their size. It is best not to tire them out completely and to return them to the water very carefully.

Anglers wanting to fish the Tangle Lakes region usually choose the Paxson entrance to the Denali Highway, as the Tangle Lakes lie only twenty miles west of Paxson on a paved road. Four-wheel-drive is not essential, but the going is slow. Services along the road are minimal and the Alaska Department of Transportation recommends carrying extra gas and two spare tires

Because of their voracious feeding habits and because their offspring are particularly vulnerable to high spring run off, the population of grayling in the Tangle River/Tangle Lakes District can be adversely effected quite quickly. The practice of catch and release contributes greatly to the preservation of these special fish of the far north.

Types of Fish
Arctic grayling, lake trout, turbot, a freshwater cod with a single whisker. Not attractive but excellent eating.

Known Hatches
Mayflies, stoneflies, caddis. Caddis prolific spring - summer, often all day. Excellent, brief hatches of black stoneflies in June.

Equipment To Use
Rods: 7 to 9 foot, 3 to 7 weight.
Reels: Click or disc to match rod.
Lines: DT or WF floating, sink-tip for lakes.
Leaders: 7 to 9 foot, 3 to 5X.
Wading or Boating: Waders and boots for rivers. Canoe, car-top boat, or float tube on lakes.

Flies to Use
Dries: Elk Hair Caddis, Black Gnat, Royal Wulff, Adams, Humpy, mosquito, Griffith's Gnat #10-14.
Nymphs: Gold Ribbed Hare's Ear, black stonefly, Zug Bug, PT, soft hackle #10-12.
Streamers: Wooly Worm, Muddler Minnow.

When to Fish
Summer - early fall is best. River grayling can be caught in early spring and late fall. Usually within a few days after ice out, fish around the edges of lakes.

Seasons & Limits
No restricted season for grayling. In 1998, grayling possession limit of 5 in this area, no size limit.

Accommodations & Services
Few and far between on the Denali Highway. Tangle Lakes Lodge and Tangle River Lodge near fishing (see appendix). Gas, lodging, and food at Cantwell or Paxson. Two campgrounds at Tangle Lakes, one at Brushkana Creek. Numerous pullouts for tents, campers, and R.V.'s.

Nearby Fly Fishing
North of Paxson and north and south of Cantwell several creeks and lakes. *Alaska Milepost*, best mile-by-mile guide to fishing the area.

Rating
The Tangle Lakes and River area rates a 10 in my book.

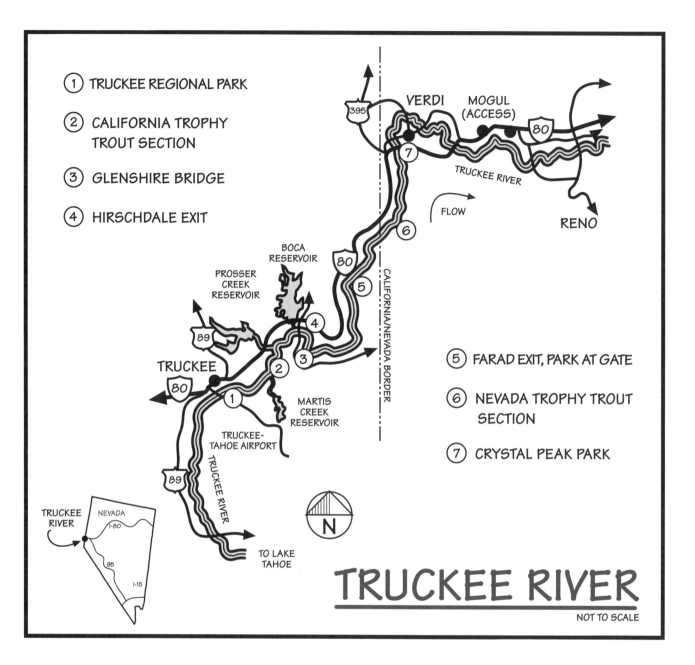

1. TRUCKEE REGIONAL PARK
2. CALIFORNIA TROPHY TROUT SECTION
3. GLENSHIRE BRIDGE
4. HIRSCHDALE EXIT

5. FARAD EXIT, PARK AT GATE
6. NEVADA TROPHY TROUT SECTION
7. CRYSTAL PEAK PARK

VERDI
MOGUL (ACCESS)
395
80
7
TRUCKEE RIVER
FLOW
6
RENO
BOCA RESERVOIR
PROSSER CREEK RESERVOIR
80
5
89
4
CALIFORNIA/NEVADA BORDER
TRUCKEE
80
3
2
MARTIS CREEK RESERVOIR
1
TRUCKEE-TAHOE AIRPORT
89
TRUCKEE RIVER
N
TRUCKEE RIVER
NEVADA
I-80
95
I-15
TO LAKE TAHOE

TRUCKEE RIVER

NOT TO SCALE

Lisa Cutter has co-owned and operated the California School of Flyfishing since 1981. She is a licensed guide and Certified Federation of Fly Fishers Fly Casting Instructor. Extremely well versed in the complexities of fly fishing, Lisa prefers to keep it simple. She's at her best with a small box of flies, a light rod, and a clear mountain stream. This uncluttered and minimalist approach to the sport seems to strike a chord with her students. A talented artist, her illustrations have appeared in numerous outdoor publications and the Sierra Trout Guide. *Lisa is an advisor to the SIMMS wader company and is on Patagonia's pro staff.*

Truckee River
California/Nevada
Lisa Cutter

*T*he Truckee is an exotic river which, technically speaking, means it flows inland and never reaches the ocean. But, to my mind, the Truckee is exotic because I can fish its waters and be completely happy never catching a fish.

Flowing from Lake Tahoe at 6,200', this freestone river tumbles and meanders its way to the high desert waters of Pyramid Lake. Even though it's paralleled most of its length by highways, byways, and train tracks, the river retains a surprisingly strong feeling of wildness, of a remote world populated only by you and its fish.

Despite all of its redeeming qualities, the Truckee can be a very fickle river. On some days the fishing can be ridiculously easy, but on other, seemingly identical days, it can be frustrating as hell. Which means that, on this river, you need to constantly experiment, play, and improvise if you wish to consistently catch fish. This is definitely NOT a cookbook fishery of routine recipes.

The average fish on the Truckee River is 10 - 14". A 16 - 18" trout is the typical "big one" for the day, and 20" plus will be the best fish of the season. Every year, anglers "in the know" catch brown trout over 10 pounds.

The Truckee's boating access is extremely limited. A few hardy souls do put in rafts, but unless you're comfortable rowing fast, narrow water, I recommend you let your feet show you the river. But, wading can also be difficult and dangerous. An uneven stream bed booby trapped, it seems, with large, sharp, slippery rocks interspersed with deep, invisible holes makes for adventuresome wading. Wading staff, felts, and cleats are strongly advised!

Because of its fickle nature, educated trout, and often difficult wading, the Truckee River isn't suited for the angler who wants easy catching. For those of us who love to fish as much as we love to catch fish, the Truckee is a jewel. Even when the fish would rather not play, a lazy day on an exotic river can do wonders for your soul.

Type of Fish
Rainbows, browns, cutthroat and trophy whitefish.

Known Hatches & Baitfish
Caddis: Glossosoma, Rhyacophila, Hydropsyche, and Dicosmoecus. Mayflies: Heptagenia, Rhithrogenia, Epeorus, Baetis, Ephemerella grandis, E. tibialis, E. inermis, and E. flavilinea. Stoneflies: Calineuria and Isogenus. Food for the big trout are sculpins and crayfish.

Equipment to Use
Rods: 9 foot, 4 to 6 weight.
Reels: Click or disc drag with a palming rim.
Lines: Weight forward floating, rarely a shooting head.
Leaders: 7 to 10 foot, 4 to 6X.
Wading: Staff, felt soled boots and cleats are a must.

Flies to Use
Dries: E/C Caddis, BiVisible Dun, mayfly cripple, Humpy, Adams, little yellow stone, ant, hopper.
Nymphs: Olive, natural, and cream Bird's Nest.
Streamers: Bugger, Goblin, Clouser, Muddler Minnow.

When to Fish
May - October. Spring and fall, fish midday. In summer, best angling generally morning and evening.

Seasons & Limits
Last Saturday in April to November 15th. Various zones of restriction, generally catch & release, barbless flies or lures. Consult recent regulations.

Accommodations & Services
Dozens of area campsites. Truckee, CA, a tourist destination along the river, has all services as does Reno, NV.

Nearby Fly Fishing
Martis Creek Reservoir, California's first catch & release, "trophy trout" lake . . . Outstanding! Hundreds of lakes and many creeks, rivers, and streams near Truckee.

Rating
The Truckee River area offers diverse fly fishing opportunities for strong, wild, and wily trout in one of the world's most beautiful mountain settings. A rock solid 8!

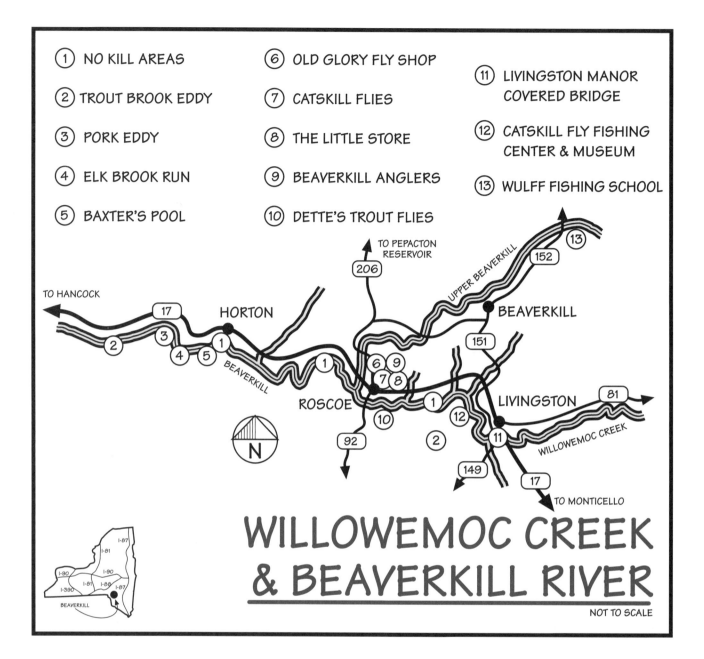

1. NO KILL AREAS
2. TROUT BROOK EDDY
3. PORK EDDY
4. ELK BROOK RUN
5. BAXTER'S POOL
6. OLD GLORY FLY SHOP
7. CATSKILL FLIES
8. THE LITTLE STORE
9. BEAVERKILL ANGLERS
10. DETTE'S TROUT FLIES
11. LIVINGSTON MANOR COVERED BRIDGE
12. CATSKILL FLY FISHING CENTER & MUSEUM
13. WULFF FISHING SCHOOL

TO PEPACTON RESERVOIR
206
TO HANCOCK
17
HORTON
UPPER BEAVERKILL
152
13
BEAVERKILL
2 3 4 5 1
BEAVERKILL
1
151
6 9
7 8
ROSCOE
1
LIVINGSTON
81
10
12
11
N
92
2
WILLOWEMOC CREEK
149
17
TO MONTICELLO

WILLOWEMOC CREEK & BEAVERKILL RIVER

NOT TO SCALE

I-87
I-81
I-90
I-90
I-390
I-81
I-88
I-87
BEAVERKILL

Misako "Misa" Ishimura is active in many conservation organizations in the United States as well as Japan, including Trout Unlimited, Japan Fly Fishers, and Trout Forum in Japan. At present, she serves as a director of three clubs: Theodore Gordon Fly Fishers, International Women Fly Fishers, and Juliana Berners Anglers. In addition, Misa conducts fly casting clinics, giving lessons in Manhattan's Central Park as well as in the Catskill Mountains of New York. In 1997, she won a NYCTU amateur casting contest and participated as a Team Japan angler in the 17th Annual World Fly Fishing Championship in Jackson Hole, Wyoming.

Willowemoc Creek & Beaverkill River
New York
Misa Ishimura

Nestled in the green Catskill Mountains within 2 hours driving distance of New York City, the area around Roscoe and Livingston Manor, New York is thought to possess some of the finest trout water in the world. For over 100 years, these clean, rich streams have enchanted writers, artists and anglers, among them Theodore Gordon, the father of modern American fly fishing. Here anglers will find not only the legendary Beaverkill River but also beautiful Willowemoc Creek.

You can fish all year in the "no-kill" stretches of these waters. Every year on the morning of April 1st, anglers from across the state converge at the Junction Pool where Beaverkill River and Willowemoc Creek meet to celebrate the opening of trout season. The day after Arbor Day marks another annual event when volunteers repair the public access to prime fishing waters on the areas creeks and rivers. Called "Project Access," this worthwhile program maintains access trails for wheelchair-bound anglers.

In July and August, if the water is not too low or too hot, try Willowemoc Creek's deeper pools or tributary inflows. Fish ants, beetles or tricos in the morning. If water levels are too low, please don't pressure the fish. For information on water levels, call Mary Dette's Hot Line (607-498-5350) or browse the Theodore Gordon Fly Fishers web site at www.tgf.org.

Fall is the best time to fish brown trout near their spawning tributaries. You'll enjoy the surprise and appreciate the pleasure of releasing the big, colorful ones. On sunny, winter afternoons, fish slower water or sections of the creek fed by springs.

Join us and discover your own "best-loved trout stream." Whenever you fish these beautiful waters, please release every wild fish you are fortunate enough to hook.

Types of Fish
Brown trout.

Known Hatches
During May and June, more than twelve different types of mayflies are hatching on the creek and river.

Equipment to Use
Rods: 9 foot, 4 to 6 weight.
Reels: Disk or click to match rod.
Lines: Weight forward or double taper floating.
Leaders: Typically 9 foot, 4 to 7X.
Wading: Easy wading, waders and boots, hippers OK.

Flies to Use
Dries: Quill Gordon, Hendrickson, march brown, gray fox, gray drake, large blue winged olive, cahill, sulphur, Baetis, caddis, as well as terrestrial and midge. It's fun to try to match the hatch with traditional, Catskill-tied, dry flies, a method of tying made popular by Winnie and Walt Dette.
Nymphs: Stone, Isonychia, and Hares Ear.
Streamers: Wooly Bugger.

When to Fish
Spring fishing on the Willowemoc can be arduous, but it is always exciting. May and June are the best months for dry fly fishing.

Season & Limits
You can fish year-round on the "no-kill" stretches.

Accommodations & Services
Restaurants, motels, campgrounds are readily available. The Fly Fishing Center and Museum hosts numerous events during the year. Call 914-439-4810, http://www.cffcm.org for more information on their upcoming programs.

Nearby Fly Fishing
The Delaware River System and other equally productive waters are very close.

Rating
In my mind, depending on the time of year, a definite 8 to 10.

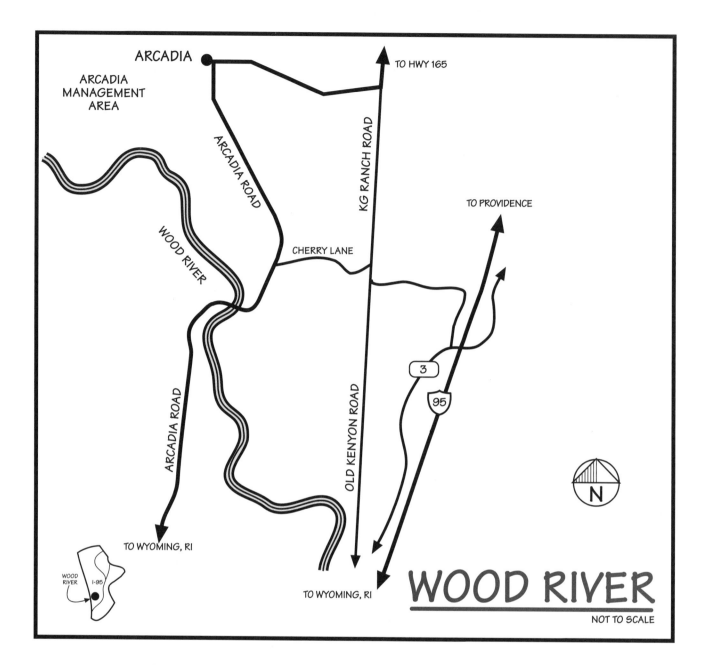

WOOD RIVER

NOT TO SCALE

Anna Minicucci, has been a fly fisher and writer, specializing in fishing, and related outdoor activities since 1965. She writes a weekly outdoor column for two newspapers, the Warwick Beacon *and the* Cranston Herald *and her work has been published in* Fly Rod & Reel *and* Outdoor Life. *Anna is also a much sought after speaker, often teaming up for these engagements with her husband, David, a master fly tier. In addition to receiving numerous writing and conservation awards, Anna is a board member of the International Women Fly Fishers and co-editor of its newsletter, a member of the Fly Fishing Business Foundation, and founder of Ladies of the Long Rod.*

Wood River
Rhode Island
Anna Minicucci

Rhode Island has received some notoriety because of the TV series, *Providence*. Despite what you might learn about my state from this melodrama, I'm here to let you in on the best kept secret about Rhode Island: its fishing, both salt and fresh water and especially the Wood River.

Not every state can boast of fresh and saltwater fishing separated, in some instances, by a mere 10 miles. You can saltwater fish in the morning, then pack up your gear and cast to Wood River trout rising to an evening hatch of mayflies, in the same day.

The Wood River winds through sylvan corridors where wildlife and flora abound. Before it eventually joins the Pawcatuck, the Wood offers the angler the complete menu of a four-star trout stream: easy access, safe wading, bubbling riffles, easy runs, and dark, deep pools that hold trophy-sized brown and rainbow trout.

From late June through August, the Wood River becomes a fly fisher's dream. In summertime, many less dedicated anglers have abandoned the river in favor of other pursuits. Hike into the High Banks and Pines sections of the river and enjoy the natural beauty of these inner reaches of the Wood River. You can also fish for native brook trout, undisturbed by a crowd of other fishers.

Traveling north or south on Route 95 through Rhode Island, anglers have a difficult choice to make. They can take Route 1A to some of the best saltwater fishing in the northeast, or they can opt for Route 3 that will take them to the Arcadia Management Area (near Exeter) and the Wood River. All dirt roads leading through the management area to the best fishing spots on the river are reasonably well maintained. Four-wheel-drive vehicles are not necessary.

Rhode Island's southern corner offers many other "saltwater near freshwater" angling experiences comparable to the Wood River. You'll just have to visit Rhode Island and find them. My sympathy goes out to anglers in other, larger states where extended driving times take away from otherwise enjoyable days of fishing.

Type of Fish
Rainbows, browns, and brookies.

Known Hatches
Mayflies, March to November. Stoneflies and caddis, March to October. Midges, year-round.

Equipment to Use
Rods: 8 to 9 foot, 4 to 6 weight.
Reels: Click or disc to match rod.
Lines: Weight forward or double taper floating and, in early spring, full sink and sink-tip.
Leaders: 7 - 9 foot, 3 to 6X.
Wading: Waders and cleated sandals or boots.
Other: Polarized sunglasses, sunscreen, billed cap, and clothing appropriate for changeable weather.

Flies to Use
Dries & Nymphs: Mayfly, stonefly, caddis, midge to match naturals in all stages of development.
Streamers: Bucktail to imitate the baitfish (fry and minnows), black and yellow marabou streamer.

When to Fish
Early morning to noon, then from late afternoon 'til dark.

Season & Limits
Trout: Second Saturday in April - February. Rt. 165 - dam, 6 fish per day. Bag limit of 2 fish on certain stretches. All Rhode Island freshwater fish are game fish. Rhode Island Fish & Game, (401-222-3075).

Accommodations & Services
Lodging and services in the town of Hope Valley. Rhode Island's Division of Tourism (800-556-2484) supplies free tourist packages, state recreational map. Web site: www.VisitRhodeIsland.com.

Nearby Fly Fishing
A two mile stretch of the Falls River is catch & release.

Rating
The Wood River rates a definite 8.

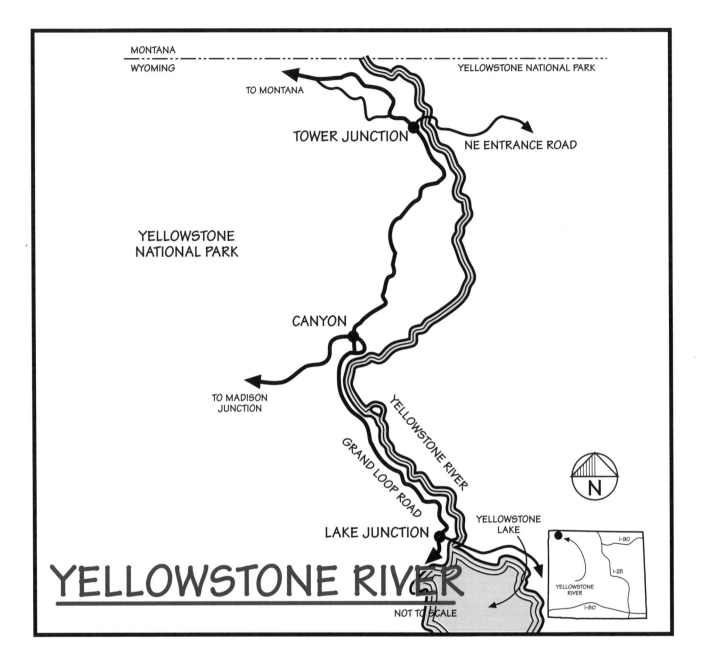

YELLOWSTONE RIVER

NOT TO SCALE

Maggie Merriman has given casting demonstrations, slide shows, and lectures to fly clubs, national conclaves and sport shows around the country for the last thirty years. She is a strong advocate of introducing women to fly fishing. From 1995 through 1998, Maggie created and ran the Federation of Fly Fishers National Women's Educational Fly Fishing Program and, in May 1998, she represented the USA Fly Fishers at the prestigious Chatsworth Angling Fair in England. She has received the FFF's President's Pin as well as the Lew Jewett and "Woman of the Year" Awards. During the summer, Maggie runs her own fly fishing schools based in West Yellowstone, Montana.

Yellowstone River
Wyoming
Maggie Merriman

America's first national park, Yellowstone was established in 1872 and quickly became a model for other such parks in the United States and around the world. It was only natural, then, that the Yellowstone River became the first in any park designated "catch and release," setting the standard for similar programs across the country.

The Yellowstone River is situated in Yellowstone National Park in the northwest corner of Wyoming. Surrounded by spectacular scenery, the river is renowned for its crystal clear water and multiple hatches. With water temperatures running from cool to cold, the Yellowstone as it runs through the park is mostly wide, flat water with some riffles here and there. But, because it is so clear, you will easily be able to spot subsurface fish as well as cast to numerous rising fish.

The Yellowstone Cutthroat is a beautiful fish, especially when it sports its spawning colors. And, thanks to the Yellowstone's special regulations, the average size of these beautiful trout has remained fairly constant over the years at 16 - 20".

Contrary to stories that circulate among anglers, Yellowstone Cutthroat are *not* easy to catch. Because the water is so clear, drag free floats are critical on this river; fish will see every angling mistake you make. These cutthroat can also be very selective. Matching the hatch, selecting the correct hook size, and casting accuracy are a must. But, if you're a novice or intermediate fly fisher, don't let me scare you away; this great river will definitely hone your skills. There probably isn't a better river to teach lessons in choosing the right fly, accurate casting, and drag free drift.

While fishing the Yellowstone River is a wonderful experience in and of itself, you should also make time to see the rest of the awesome natural setting it flows through. For the best sightseeing, I recommend the lower loop through the park. If you have time, you might also consider short trips to other noteworthy places such as the Grand Teton area around Jackson Hole or the famous Western and Indian Museums in Cody, Wyoming.

Types of Fish
Yellowstone Cutthroat: the ONLY place they exist!

Known Hatches
A rich stream with many hatches. Check with the local fly shops for current hatches.

Equipment to Use
Rods: 8 to 9 foot, 3 to 5 weight.
Reels: Click or disc trout reel to match rod.
Lines: Weight forward or double taper floating.
Leaders: 9 foot, 5 to 7X.
Wading: Chest waders with felt soled boots. Most of the river has a gravel bottom and wades easily. During early season high water, only wade in a bit above your knees. Wait until later in the season to wade deeper.

Flies to Use
Dries: Elk Hair Caddis, parachute Adams, what's hatching.
Nymphs: Prince, Hare's Ear, Zug Bug.
Streamers: Leech and Wooly Bugger.

When to Fish
Fishing can be great from opening day until mid-October.

Seasons & Limits
Fish Sulphur Caldron to a few miles south of La Hardy Rapids, July 15 to mid-Oct. Catch & release, single barbless hook only.

Accommodations & Services
Food, gas, and lodging 20 -30 minutes from Yellowstone Lake or River. Full services 1 - 1 1/2 hour away in West Yellowstone, MT, Jackson Hole or Cody, WY. More information: Maggie Merriman Fly Fishing Schools (May to October, 406-646-7824. October to May, 714-969-5829).

Nearby Fly Fishing
In Yellowstone Park the Madison, Firehole, and Gibbon rivers and Yellowstone Lake.

Rating
Used to be a 10 plus. Yellowstone Cutthroat have declined due to the lake trout in Yellowstone Lake. Currently, 6 or 7.

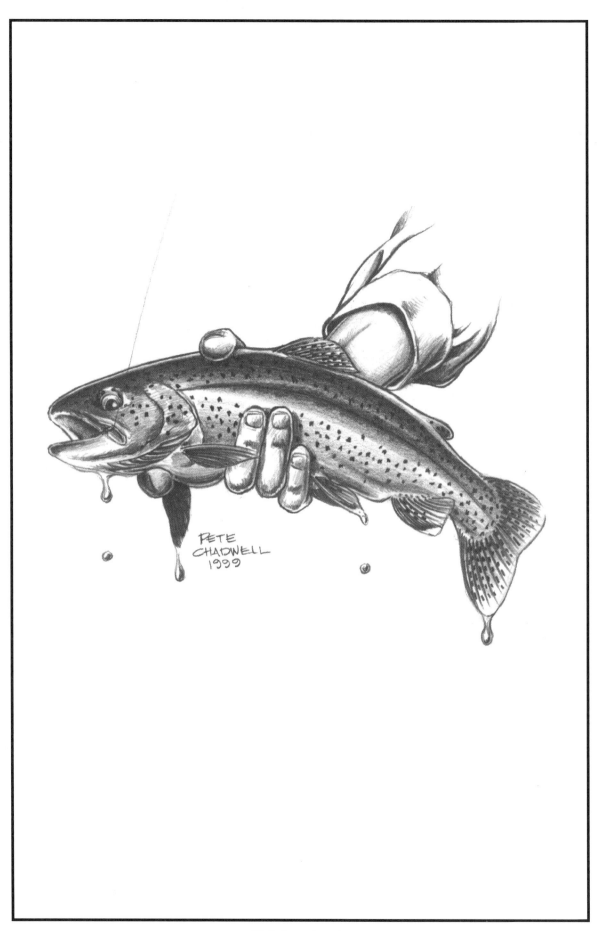

Rainbow trout.

Appendix

Additional
Fly Fishing Information

Arkansas
Norfork River
Mountain Home
Best Western (870-425-6001), Holiday Inn (870-425-5101), Norfork Inn (870-425-1544), Ramada Inn (870-425-9191), Comfort Inn (870-424-9000), Super 8 Motel (870-424-5600). Norfork, Peals Resort (870-499-5215), Schroder Haus B & B (870-499-7775).

Quarry State Park Campground (870-425-2700).

Blue Ribbon Flies, 1340 Highway 5 S.
Mountain Home, AR 72653
(640-425-0447)

Fishermens Annex, 313 Highway 62 E.
Mountain Home, AR 72653
(640-425-6848)

1-800-ASK-FISH (275-3474)

Alaska
Contact Creek
Alaska Net & Supply Inc
King Salmon, AK 99613
(907-439-5137)

Rod and Reel
701 W 36th Ave
Anchorage, AK 99503
(907-561-0662)

Custom Rod & Tackle
3200 Spenard Rd
Anchorage, AK 99503
(907-258-3474)

Tangle River
Pudge Kleinkauf web site, http://www.halcyon.com/wffn/. PO Box 243-963, Anchorage, AK 99524. Services along the Denali Highway are few and far between. Gas, lodging, food at Cantwell or Paxson at either end of the highway, precious little in between. Two lovely campgrounds at Tangle Lakes, one spread out on a high ridge above the lake and another smaller one nestled right along the river. There are numerous pull-outs all along the highway, and tents, campers, and recreational vehicles park in many of them while their inhabitants hike, bike, fish, or bird watch. Only one other real campground along the entire rest of the road, the comfortable but often overcrowded, 17-site, Brushkana Creek campground.

Gary Kings
202 E Northern Lights
Anchorage, AK 99503
(907)272-5401

McAfees Fly Shop
750 W Diamond Blvd.
Anchorage, AK 99515
(907)344-1617

Baja, Mexico
Bahia De Las Palmas
Baja on the Fly
P.O. Box 81961 San Diego CA 92138
(800-919-225) Fax (619-223 5080)
Mexico (011-52-114-82-1-79)
www.bajafly.com
bajafly@usa.net

Minerva's Baja Tackle
Cabo San Lucas B.C.S.
(114-31282) Fax (114-30440)
email:minervas@1cabonet.com.mx
www.mexonline.com/minervas.htm
Guide Service
Bajaanglers.com
Baja Travel Information
www.discoverbaja.com
www.vagabundos.com
www.bajanet.com
www.bajasun.com/
www.bajalife.com/index.htm
www.trybaja.com
www.baja.net
www.bajalinks.com
Rancho Buena Vista
(1-800-919-2252)
hotelbvbr@aol.com
Hotel Buena Vista Beach & Resort
www.hotelbuenavista.com
http://members.aol.com/Thronsen/index.html (Rancho Buena Vista)
Rancho Leonero
www.bajafly.com/leonero.htm
Las Arenas Hotel
www.lasarenas.com.html
Los Barilles Hotel

www.bajafly.com/motel/index.html
Hotel Palmas de Cortez, Punta Colorado, Playa del Sol
www.bajaresort.com
Baja Information Center
www.bajafly.com/bbs799
www.bajafly.com/Spabv.htm
www.bajafly.com/motel/index.html
Baja Maps
www.sandiego-online.com/baja/maps/6areas.htm
Cabo Weather
www.loscabosguide.com/weather.htm

California
Big Pine Creek
Bell's Sporting Goods & Hardware
Lee Vining, CA 93541 (619-647-6406)

Ken's Alpine Shop & Sporting Goods
258 Main Street Bridgeport, CA 93517
(619-932-7707)

Trout Fitter, Shellmart # 3
Mammoth Lakes, CA (619- 924-3676)

Yosemite Angler, 49er Shopping Center
Mariposa, CA 95350 (209-966-8377)

Village Sport Shop
Yosemite Park, CA (209-372-1286)

Buz's Fly & Tackle. 400 N. Johnson Ave.
Visalia, CA 93291 (209-734-1151)

Hot Creek, Mammoth Lakes Area
Visitors Bureau (800-367-6572)

Orvis San Francisco
300 Grant Avenue
San Francisco, CA 94108
(415-392-1600)

Bell's Sporting Goods & Hardware
Lee Vining, CA (619-647-6406)

Ken's Alpine Shop & Sporting Goods
258 Main Street, Bridgeport, CA
(619-932-7707)

Truckee River
Truckee, California is a tourist destination with an abundance of motels, hotels, and rentals. Popular spots, Best Western (530-587-4525), Donner Lake Village Resort (800-621-6664), Northstar at Tahoe (530-562-2248). Truckee area has over 24 local eateries, Lisa Cutter's current favorite is Pianeta's (530-587-4694).

Donner State Park, Donner Lake
(800-444-7275)

Ralph & Lisa Cutter's California
School of Fly fishing
PO Box 8212, Truckee, CA 96162
(1-800-58TROUT)

Truckee River Outfitters
10200 Donner Pass Rd.
Truckee, CA 96161 (530-582-0900)

Mountain Hardware
11320 Donner Pass Rd.
Truckee, CA 96161 (530-582-4844)

Reno Fly Shop
294 E. Moana Lane #14
Reno, NV 89502 (702-825-3474)

Canada, British Columbia
Stellako River
Stellako Lodge
Box 400, Fraser Lake B.C. VOT ISO
April - Oct. (250-699-6695)

Par Three Sports, Fraser Lake
(250-699-8063)

Colorado
Division of Regulatory Agencies for Guides and Outfitters (303-894-7778)

Colorado Div. Of Wildlife
(303-297-1192)

Arkansas River
Browner's Fly Shop
Buena Vista (719-395-6133)

Browner's Fly Shop
3745 E. Highway 50, Salida
(800-826-6505)

Arkansas River Fly Shop
7500 Highway 50, Salida
(719-539-3474)

Eagle River
Cindy Scholl at Gorsuch Outfitters
263 Gore Creek Dr.
Vail, CO 81657 (970-476-2294)
(1-877-476-4700)
E-mail, scholls@sni.net

Mountain Angler
311 S. Main St. Breckenridge, CO 80424
(970-453-4665)

South Platte River
Flies & Lies (on the S. Platte)
Deckers, CO (303- 647-2237)

Pikes Peak Angler
119 N. Tejon Street
Colorado Springs, CO 80903
(719-636-3348)

Denver Angler, 5455 W 38th Ave.
Denver, CO 8021 (303-455-1353)

Trout Fisher, 2020 S. Parker Rd.
Denver, CO 80231 (303-369-7970)

Florida
Florida Game & Fish Commission
(904-488-1960)

County Maps
Florida Department of Transportation
605 Suwannee Street, #12
Tallahassee, FL 32399-0450

Islamorada
Abels Tackle Box
8484341 Old Hwy Islamorada, FL 33037
(305-664-2521)

Bluewater World
460 Overseas Hwy Key Largo, FL 33037
(305-451-2511) Bluewaterworld.Com

Bud 'N Mary's Marina
14315 Overseas Hwy
Islamorada, FL 33036 (305-664-4864)

Florida Keys Outfitters
16384 Overseas Hwy
Islamorada, FL 33036 (305-664-5423)

Fly Fisherman
1114 S Washington Ave.
Titusville, FL 32780 (407-267-0348)

Islamorada Tackle
16114 Overseas Hwy
Islamorada, FL 33036 (305-664-4578)

World Wide Sportsman
16709 Overseas Hwy
Islamorada, FL 33036 (305-664-4615)

Massachusetts
Martha's Vineyard
M.V. Chamber of Commerce
(508-693-0085)
"Martha's Vineyard On Line",
www.mvol.com: hotels, car rental, real estate, fishing guides, tackle shops.

There are five towns on Martha's Vineyard, each with its own character and variety of hotels, houses to rent, and fly shops. Vineyard Haven and Edgartown have two public boat launches, Gay Head has one. Canoe and Kayak rentals at Winds Up, Vineyard Haven. Larry's Tackle Shop and Coop's (Edgartown) are the main fly shops. Two women guides on the island are IGFA world record holders: Capt. Leslie Smith (Backlash Charters) and Lori Vanderlaske. Capt. Karen Kukolich holds IGFA fly rod records and teaches casting.

Montana
Gallatin River
Gallatin Riverguides
Highway 191
Big Sky, MT 59716 (406-995-2290)

East Slope Anglers
Highway 191
Big Sky, MT 59716 (406-995-4369)

Bob Ward & Sons,
2320 W Main St.
Bozeman, MT 59718 (406-586-4381)

Montana Troutfitters Orvis
1716 W Main St. Bozeman, MT 59715
(406-587-4707)

Rivers Edge
2012 N. 7th Ave. Bozeman, Mt 5971
(406-586-5373)

Madison River
Campfire Lodge
8500 Hebgen Lake Road
West Yellowstone, MT 59758-9718
(406-646-7258)
May - Sept., cabins and campsites with full hook-ups. Chuck and Nancy Sperry operate a clean, well-organized resort. Small store and a café open 7:00 a.m. to 2:00 p.m., tasty riverside dining.

Yellowstone River
Maggie Merriman Fly Fishing Schools
May to October - P. O. Box 755
West Yellowstone, MT 59758
(406-646-7824)
October to May - 19191 Coastline Lane
Huntington Beach, CA (714-969-5829)

Missouri
Lake Taneycomo
River Run Outfitters
212 S. Commercial Street
Branson, MO 65616 (877-699-FISH)
(417-332-0460)
email:shop@riverrunoutfitters
www.riverrunoutfitters.com

New Mexico
San Juan River
High Desert Angler
435 S. Guadalupe, Santa Fe, NM 87501
(505-98TROUT)

New Mexico Dept. of Game & Fish
Fisheries Division (505-827-7905)

New Mexico Dept. Of Tourism
P.O. Box 20003, Santa Fe, NM 87503
(1-800-545-2040)

New York
Beaverkill River
Dette Trout Flies
P.O. Box 108
Roscoe, NY 12776
(607-498-4991)
email: ffonfamgaol.com

New York Harbor
Fly fishing guide: Capt. Joe Shastay
(201-451-1988) or (973-239-1988)
Helpfull fly & tackle shops:
New York City
Orvis (212-697-3133)
Urban Angler (212-979-7600)
Long Island
Camp-Site Sport Shop (516-271-4969)
Croton Watershed
Bedford Sportsman (914-666-8091)
Catskills
Dettes, April-October (607-498-4991)
New Jersey
Ramsey Outdoor Store (201-261-5000)
Pennsylvania
Dunkelbergers (717-421-7950)

Theodore Gordon Flyfishers web site,
links to others including IWFF members
fly fishing pages: www.tgf.org.

Register your e-mail address with NYC
Trout Unlimited, receive notice of activities: nyctu@hotmail.com

Willowemoc River
Mary Dette's Hot Line (607-498-5350)
or browse the Theodore Gordon Fly Fishers web site at www.tgf.org.

The Fly Fishing Center and Museum
(914-439-4810), www.cffcm.org, information on upcoming programs.

North Carolina
Bullhead Creek
Stone Mt. State Park information
Jesse Brown's Outdoors (704-556-0020)

Stone Mountain State Park
3042 Frank Parkway,
Roaring Gap, NC 28668.

The Outer Banks
Fishing Unlimited
7665 S Virginia Dare Trail
Nags Head, NC 27959
(919-441-5028)

Tatems Tackle Box
Nags Head, NC 27959
(919-441-7346)

Oregon
Crooked River
Oregon Dept. Of Tourism
(541-378-6254)

Oregon Dept. Fish & Game
Prineville, OR (541-477-5111)

Fishing In Oregon, Casali and Diness
Flying Pencil Publications

The Fly Fisher's Place
230 West Main St.
Sisters, OR 97759
(541-549-3474)

Fin'N'Feather
785 West 3rd Street
Prineville, OR 97754
(541-447-8691)

Rhode Island
Wood River
Rhode Island Fish & Game
(401-222-3075)

South Carolina
Hilton Head
Hilton Head Island Tide Charts
Tidelog, Southeastern Edition
(1-800-935-9666)

Tide & Current for Windows
Nautical Software Products
(1-800-946-2877)

Purchase nautical charts at most
marina's. Get *Port Royal Sound and Inland Passages,* nautical chart #11516.

Low Country Outfitters
1533 Fording Island Rd. #-316
Hilton Head Island, SC 29926
(803-837-6100)

The Westin Resort (1-800-WESTIN)
Ocean Palms Villas (1-800-228-3000)
Hyatt (1-800-55HYATT)
Main Street Inn (1-800-471-3001)
Palm Key Lodge (1-800-228-8420)

Restaurants:
Sunset Grill (843-684-6744), L'Etoile
Verte (843-785-9777), Kurama (843-
785-4955), Neno's (843-342-2400), Big
Bad Wolf (BBQ) (843-342-2933),
Hudson's (843-681-2772), Captain Sea-
food (843-686-3200), Charleston (843-
785-5008), Crazy Crab (843-363-2722)

Tennessee
Hiwassee River
Mountain Stream Cabins, 5 mins. from
river, kitchens, fireplaces, hot tubs.
(423-338-1070)
mtnscabins@ wingnet.net

Southern Memories, 20 mins. from river,
inn or cabins with kitchens.
(423-338-4351)

Rose Hill Inn (B&B) 35 mins. from river,
15 mins. from Ocoee.
(1-888-813-ROSE)
earth.vol.com/~rosehill

Hiwassee Outfitters, cabins, camping,
raft rentals, fly shop and guides.
(800-338-8133)

Riverside, Reliance, cabins, camping,
raft rental, grill, fly shop, guides.
(423-338-8115)
hiwassee@wingnet.net

Adam's Fly Shop (423-338-2162)
Hiwassee Angler & Guide Service (423-338-6000)
Little River Outfitters (423-448-9459)
Clinch River Outfitters (423-494-0972)

Attractions: The International Olympic Ocoee River, John Muir Trail, Nancy Ward Grave site, Chilhowee Glider Port, Swift Aircraft Museum, Reliance Historic District, including Webb's Store and Raft Service, Hiwassee Union Church, Higdon Hotel.

Licenses: nonresident 3 day, $20.50, 10 day, $30.50, annual, $51.00.

State Regulations: Coast Guard approved floatation devices for each individual in or on a water craft. $2 Per car, per day parking fee on Cherokee National Forest Service Road 108 from Taylor's Island to the powerhouse. No alcohol in the park or on the river.

1-800-ASK-FISH (275-3474)

Texas
Llano River
Raye Carrington on theLlano River
HC 10 Box 40
Mason, TX 76856
fax (915-347-9009)
raye@carrington.com

Austin Angler
312 Congress Ave.
Austin, TX 78701
(512-472-4553)

Anglers Edge Inc
3926 Westheimer Rd.
Houston, TX 77027
(713-993-9981)

Orvis Co.
5848 Westheimer Rd.
Houston, TX 77057
(713-783-2111)

Canoesport
5808 S. Rice Ave.
Houston, TX 77081
(713-660-7000)

Utah
Logan River
Rainys Flies & Supplies
690 N. 100 E.
Logan, UT 84321
(801-753-6766)

Traders Den, 434 S Main St.
Logan, UT 84321
(801-752-8004)

Bear Lake Motor Lodge
50 S Bear Lake Blvd.
Garden City, UT 84028
(801-946-8892)

Sweetwater Ideal Beach Resort
2176 S Bear Lake Blvd.
Garden City, UT 84028
(801-946-3364)

Western Rivers Flyfisher
1071 East 900 S.
Salt Lake City, UT 84105
(800-545-4312)

Virginia
Sweet Springs Creek
Beaver Falls Dam Farm (540-559-2622), e-mail:bgoodwin@cfw.com for specific directions. Be sure to tell them Rhea Topping sent you. Try Old Earlehurst B&B, Milton Hall, Callahan; The Greenbriar Hotel, The Wylie House, White Sulphur Springs; The Homestead, Hot Springs.

Wisconsin
Knapp River
Seven Pines Lodge
1098 340th Ave.
Frederic, WI 54837
(715-653-2323)

Rod fee $23 half day, $36 full day for river access. Season membership $400, guides and clinics available by reservation. The lodge provides four-course meals to guests and to the public by reservation. Call ahead for rod/fishing reservations. Many other hotels and motels within 40 minutes.

Wyoming
Flat Creek
Jackson Hole
Chamber of Commerce
(307-733-3316)

Crescent H Ranch
Box 347 K,
Wilson, WY 83014
(307-733-3674)

Westbank Angler
Teton Village, WY 83025
(307-733-6483)

Jack Dennis Sports
P.O. Box 3369
Jackson, WY 83001
(307-737-3270)

High Country Flies
P.O. Box 3432
Jackson, WY 83001
(307-733-7210)

Orvis Jackson Hole
485 W. Broadway
Jackson, WY 83001
(307-733-5407)

Snake River
Reel Women Fly Fishing Outfitters
P.O. Box 289
Victor, ID 83455
(208-787-2657)
Fax (208-787-2691)
reelwomen1@aol.com
www.reel-women.com

1-800-ASK-FISH (275-3474)
in DC, TN, ME, AZ, AR, ID, Ill, WI, KS, MI, MS, OK, UT.

Casting For Recovery
Chairwoman, Gwenn Perkins
Vice-Chair, Margot Page
Program Director, Susan Balch
(888-553-3500)

Administrative Offices
PMB 257
946 Great Plains Avenue
Needham, MA 02492
e-mail: fishlady@sover.net

Women's Fly Fishing Clubs

Courtesy of Cecilia Kleinkauf
Women's Fly Fishing
www.halcyon.com/wffn/orwrit

International Women Fly Fishers
Jodi Pate, President
E-mail: fishinPate@aol.com

Betsey French, Vice President
E-mail:betsey@montanaflyfishing.com

Pudge Kleinkauf, Secretary
E-mail: ckleinkauf@micronet.net

Yvonne Graham, Membership
P.O. Box 81961 San Diego, CA 92138
(800) 919-2252
E-mail: bajafly@aol.com

Pat Magnuson, Membership
E-mail: emagnuson@earthlink.net

www.sisteranglers.com
Fly fishing information and discussion
center for women, by women.
e-mail:sisteranglers@usa.net

Arizona
Dame Juliana Anglers
510 W. Willetta Street
Phoenix, AZ 85003
juliana@azoutbackanglers.com
www.azoutbackanglers.com/Dame.html
Seminars with women instructors, outings, conservation projects, activities.

California
Golden West Women Flyfishers
790 27th Avenue
San Francisco, CA 94121
kreiger@aimnet.com

The Irresistibles
2042 Alexander Dr.
Escondido, CA 92025

The Ladybugs Fly Fishing Club
3340 Lariat Drive
Cameron Park, CA 95682
www.theladybugs.com
fishen@directcon.net
Fly fishing trips, lessons, speakers, fly
tying, monthly meetings.

Colorado
Colorado Women Flyfishers
P.O. Box 46035,
Denver, CO 80201
tita@ballardspahr.com
A sociable organization for women who
fly fish. Have fun, enjoy
camaraderie of other women fly fishers.
Meetings first Tuesday of each month
(except July & December).

Delaware
Delaware Valley Women's Fly Fishing
Association
711 Fairview Ave.
Wilmington, DE 19809
oreflyfish@aol.com
A friendly environment for women to
learn the art of fly fishing.

Florida
Tampa Bay Fly Fishing Club
10424 Raffia Dr.
Port Richey, FL 34668

Emerald Coast Fly Rodders
P.O. Box 1131
Ft. Walton Beach, FL 32549
rdarby3@ix.netcom.com

Georgia
Georgia Women Flyfishers
(formerly Reel Women of Georgia)
1003 Muirfield Drive
Marietta, GA 30068
www.accessatlanta.com/community/
groups/gawomfly/index.html
GaWomFly@aol.com
To introduce and educate women in the
sport of fly fishing in a supportive, non-
competitive environment, to fish and to
have fun! Meetings second Monday of
every month.

Maine
Tacky Women's Angler Team
P.O. Box 1
Anson, ME 04911
trueview@somtel.com

Maryland
Chesapeake Women Anglers
35 Freeman Circle
Port Deposit, MD 21904
sueggert@dpnet.net
Clinics for beginning fly fishers, fresh
and saltwater trips, classes and a supportive atmosphere for women who love the
sport.

Michigan
Flygirls
P.O. Box 828
Pentwater, MI 49449
www.fedflyfishers.org/flygirls.htm
jdschramm@oceana.net
Networking, fishing outings, learning
events, newsletter, breast cancer
recovery retreats, mentoring.

Minnesota
Women Anglers of Minnesota
P.O. Box 580653
Minneapolis, MN 55468

Montana
Missoula Flyfishers
650 Big Flat Rd.
Missoula, MT 59801

New Jersey
Delaware Valley
Women's Fly Fishing Association
711 Fairview Ave.
Wilmington, DE 19809
oreflyfish@aol.com
A friendly and supportive environment
for women to learn the art of fly fishing
in cold, warm, and saltwater.

Fish 'n Chicks
P.O. Box 923
Far Hills, NJ 07931

New Mexico
She Fishes!
3214 Mathews N.E.
Albuquerque, NM 87501
shadowbot@aol.com
Dedicated to the enhancement of fishing among women through experiences,
expertise, fishing relationships, and eth-
ics and conservation.

New York
Julianna Berner's Anglers
31 Pumpkin Cay Road, #A
Key Largo, FL 33037
www1.shore.net/~bjfeibel/juliana.html
nanzakon@aol.com

Oregon
The Damsel Flies
3800 N. Delta Hwy.
Eugene, OR 97408

The Lady Anglers
High Desert Chapter
P.O. Box 1253
Umatilla, OR 97882

The Lady Anglers Fishing Society
Portland Chapter
17084 S. Monroe Street
Mulino, OR 97042

Pennsylvania
Delaware Valley
Women's Fly Fishing Association
711 Fairview Ave.
Wilmington, DE 19809
oreflyfish@aol.com

Rhode Island
Ladies of the Long Rod
203 Sterling Ave.
Providence, RI 02909
awriter203@earthlink.net

Tennessee
Tennessee Brookies
c/o Linda Good Retreats
4046 Outer Drive
Nashville, TN 37204
RETREATS@aol.com

Texas
Women in Waders
4030 Moorhead
Corpus Christi, TX 78410
Dragon_Lady613@yahoo.com
Meets first Wednesday of the month. Salt
and fresh water trips.

Utah
The Lady Anglers Fishing Society
Utah Chapter
992 Halycon Dr.
Murray, UT 84123

Damselfly
appleday@earthlink.net
Provides opportunities to meet other fishing women while fishing.

Washington
Northwest Women Flyfishers
P.O. Box 31020
Seattle, WA 98103
GJR24760@aol.com

Wisconsin
Wisconsin Sportswomen Club
W237 N 1480 Busse Rd.
Waukesha, WI 53188

Common Game Fish
Found in Most Waters in This Guidebook

CUTTHROAT TROUT

Dark green on back, yellow or pink sides with black spots. Red slash under jaw.

BROWN TROUT

Brown back with large black spots. Red spots on sides with gray-blue halos.

RAINBOW TROUT

The most abundant wild and hatchery fish. An olive-bluish back with black spots. Sides have light red or pink band.

BROOK TROUT

Black, blue-gray or green back, mottled light colored markings. Sides have red spots with blue halos. Square tail. Lower fins red, striped with black and white. Prefers colder water.

LAKE TROUT

Dark greenish-brown back and sides with irregular light-colored spots and deeply forked tail. Also called "Mackinaw Trout."

GRAYLING

In the whitefish family. Silvery gray with black spots. Very large dorsal fin spotted with blue and edged with pink. Ventral fins are striped with purple.

LARGEMOUTH BASS

Green back, silvery sides, large irregular spots. Soft dorsal fin separated from spiny dorsal fin.

SMALLMOUTH BASS

Dark brown back with vertical bronze stripes on sides. Spiny dorsal fin (9-10 spines) soft dorsal fin joined to spiny dorsal fin.

BLUEGILL

Mottled blue and green with orange or red breast. Large black spot on gill cover.

ASIATIC CARP

Dark brown back, fading to golden brown on flanks.

NORTHERN PIKE

Blue-ish to gray-green back with yellow to light gold spots in irregular rows. Long slender body, duck-billed snout and sharp teeth.

BONEFISH

Brownish Silver above, white underneath. Common in shallow lagoons and estuaries. Fair fighter. Taken on shrimp and crab patterns.

SEA TROUT

Brownish Silver above, white underneath. Common in shallow lagoons and estuaries. Fair fighter. Taken on shrimp and crab patterns.

ROOSTERFISH

Dark gray back, silver sides, pronounced diagonal stripes, comblike dorsal fin.

CABRILLA

1 - 10 lbs. Variety of colors and sub species. Usually found around rock structure.

BLACK SNOOK

2 - 40 lbs. Inshore, beaches with dirty water, lagoons. Bluish back, silver sides, black lateral line.

STRIPED BASS

Greenish back, 7-8 horizontal stripes on silver background on sides.

ALBACORE

Up to nearly 100 lbs. Blue back and silvery sides. Easily identified by the very long pectoral fin and yellow finlets

REDFISH

Dark reddish-brown back fades to a pale rust color. Conspicuous large "eyespot" near tail.

TARPON

Up to 150 lbs and beyond. Greenish back with brilliant metallic flanks and very large scales.

Common Flies
Used In Most Waters In This Guidebook

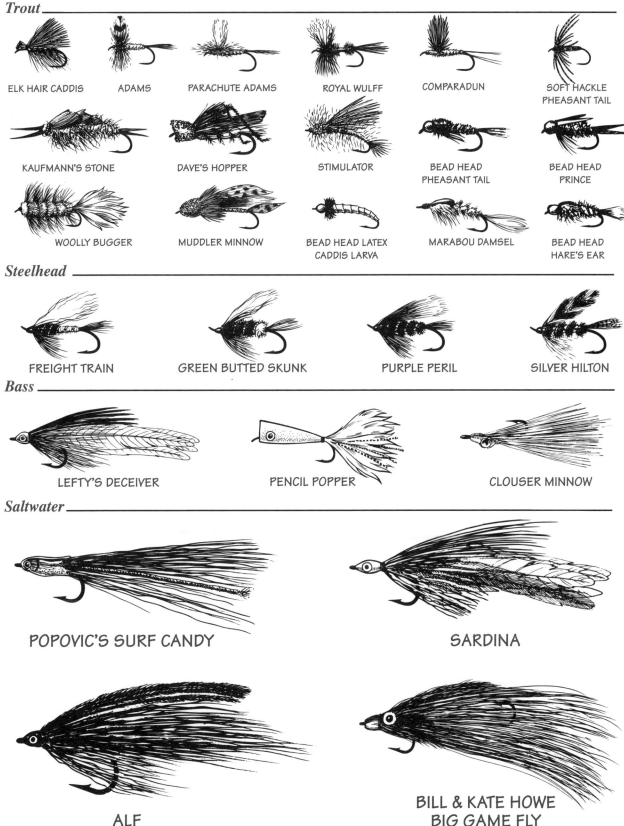

Trout

ELK HAIR CADDIS ADAMS PARACHUTE ADAMS ROYAL WULFF COMPARADUN SOFT HACKLE PHEASANT TAIL

KAUFMANN'S STONE DAVE'S HOPPER STIMULATOR BEAD HEAD PHEASANT TAIL BEAD HEAD PRINCE

WOOLLY BUGGER MUDDLER MINNOW BEAD HEAD LATEX CADDIS LARVA MARABOU DAMSEL BEAD HEAD HARE'S EAR

Steelhead

FREIGHT TRAIN GREEN BUTTED SKUNK PURPLE PERIL SILVER HILTON

Bass

LEFTY'S DECEIVER PENCIL POPPER CLOUSER MINNOW

Saltwater

POPOVIC'S SURF CANDY SARDINA

ALF BILL & KATE HOWE BIG GAME FLY

Easy Field Guide
Fly Fishing Terms
Especially for the Beginner

Action The relative resistance to bending as you move down the length of a particular fly rod.

Anti-Reverse Reel Reel handle does not spin when line is pulled from reel.

Attractor A fly designed to attract attention and look like something good to eat.

Backing A very strong, thin braided line tied to the fly reel and to which you attach the fly line itself.

Barbless A type of hook which does not have a barb on the pointed end. Research shows barbless hooks hold as well if tension is kept on the line by the fisher.

Beadhead A nymph or wet fly which has a small brass or chrome bead placed on the hook ahead of the fly pattern.

Bimini Twist A knot that creates a loop with shock absorption.

Bite Tippet 12" of heavier line at the end of the class tippet to prevent a fish with teeth or a bill from breaking the line.

Blood Knot Ties tippet material to the end of a leader.

Bluegill A small, warmwater sunfish.

Brook Trout (Salvelinus fontinalis) A trout-like fish indigenous to the Northeast and Midwest United States. Not a trout, a member of the Char family.

Brown Trout (Salmo trutta) A trout originally indigenous to Europe, Brown Trout can now be found all over America and Canada, as well as many other countries in the world.

Caddis Fly (Order Trichoptera) A very common waterborne insect with wings held back and up at a 45 degree angle.

Catch & Release The practice of releasing all fish caught unharmed. It is based on a value that the fishing experience is more important than keeping fish.

Char (Salvelinus) American Brook Trout and Lake Trout are Char found in the United States. Char are cousins of trout, and breed with them, but their offspring are sterile.

Clouser A fly with weighted eyes which allows it to sink quicker and swim with the hook point up.

Cranefly The "Daddy Longlegs" of flying insects, fished mainly as a terrestrial, late summer and early fall.

Cutthroat Trout (Oncorhynchus clarki) Originally indigenous to the Western drainages of the Rocky Mountains, it has red throat slashes under its jaw.

Damselfly (Enallagma cyathigarum) A large aquatic fly with a long skinny, blue thorax and wings that are held back at an angle.

Direct Drive Reel The handle spins as line comes off.

Disk Drag A mechanical method of applying resistance to fly line as it is drawn out by a fish that is hooked.

Dolly Varden A Char that often runs to the sea.

Double Haul A casting technique with a pulling in and releasing of line during both backcast and forward cast.

Dun The stage of a waterborne insect just after it has emerged and has the ability to fly.

Emerger That stage when a waterborne insect leaves its shuck and emerges into a flying insect.

False Cast The act of forecasting and backcasting without ever delivering the fly to the water.

Ferrule The method used to join two sections of a fly rod.

Floating Line A fly line that is designed not to sink.

Fly Line The thick-bodied line attached to the backing, which is used to actually cast the fly.

Fry A baby fish.

Grayling (Thymallus thymallus) An elegant looking member of the salmonid family of fish that looks like a silver colored trout (but isn't a trout) and has a very large dorsal (top) fin.

Hatch The time when a species of waterborne insect is emerging and becoming a flying insect.

Clinch Knot Ties a fly to the end of a leader or tippet.

Lake Trout (Salvelinus namaycush) Not trout but members of the Char family that live and spawn in lakes.

Leader A thin, clear tapered line attached to the end of the fly line, to which either the tippet or fly is attached.

Line Class The breaking strength of the class tippet or leader.

Loading The act of bending a fly rod at the end of a back cast, caused by the weight of the fly line transferring weight into stored energy held in the waterborne insect with wings in a near vertical position.

Mend To move the fly line upstream from the fly.

Midge (Diptera) A very small, mosquito-like fly.

Nail Knot Ties backing to fly line and leader to the fly line.

Nymph Undeveloped insect that lives under the water prior to emerging into a winged insect.

Pack Rod A fly rod that breaks down into 3 to 6 pieces, that easily packs while traveling or into remote areas.

Palming Using the palm to apply pressure on the reel.

More Fly Fishing Terms

Panga An open skiff with or without a bait tank.

Pool A location in a stream where the water is deeper and runs slower than most other locations.

Popper A floating lure used for warm and salt water fish.

Polarized Sun Glasses Specially tinted glasses that reduce glare, allow you to see into the water, get protection from UV rays and hooks. Use amber or yellow in low light, gray in strong light.

Rainbow Trout (Oncorhynchus mykiss) Indigenous to Pacific drainages of the Rocky Mountains, known by a rich pinkish color along the fishes side.

Reach Cast A Cast which is used when fishing downstream or when your need extra slack in your line.

Rest the Water Allowing water to calm down after a disturbance.

Rise A fish coming to the surface and feeding.

Roll Cast Used where there is little room for a backcast.

Run A location in a stream with shallow running water over a rocky streambed that feeds into a pool.

Salmon Large fish which hatch in fresh water and migrate to a lake or the ocean. Some return to the stream of their origin to spawn and then die.

Scud Small cold water crustaceans that look like a shrimp.

Sea Run Fresh water trout that migrate to the sea, grow to adulthood, then return to their natal waters to spawn.

Shooting Head The weighted, forward section of the fly line which casts farther.

Shooting Head System Fly line with the shooting head and running line attached with a knot, not seamless.

Shooting Line Releasing extra line held in the free hand as the line passes the caster in the forecast.

Shooting Taper Used to describe a rather short (45-46') fly line with a majority of the weight out at the front end.

Sink Tip A weighted portion of line used with floating line that permits the tip to sink.

Single Action A fixed drag fly reel, that cannot be adjusted.

Spinner The final stage of a waterborne insect during the mating session, when it falls to the water and dies.

Spinner Fall When many thousands of waterborne insects like Mayflies and Caddis Flies fall and die.

Spring Creek A stream that originates from water coming up from the ground, as opposed to a freestone stream which originates from run-off or snow melt.

Streamer A fly representing baitfish, fished subsurface.

Steelhead A type of Rainbow Trout that migrates from the stream in which it is hatched to the ocean or a large landlocked lake.

Stocker Hatchery raised fish placed in a water for fishing.

Stonefly (Order Plecoptera) A large aquatic fly that emerges by crawling out of the water onto a rock, splits its shuck and becomes a flying insect.

Streamer A fly that imitates a small fish, worm, leech, etc.

Strike Indicator Floating foam or yarn, attached to the leader above a nymph or other wet fly.

Strip Retrieving fly line with the hand not holding the rod.

Structure Large objects in water, such as big rocks, trees, dock pilings, etc., around which fish stay.

Surgeon's Knot Used to attach tippet to the end of a leader.

Tail Out The end of a stream pool, where it again becomes shallow, fast-moving water over a rocky or sandy bottom.

Tailwaters A river that's fed from the bottom of a dam.

Terrestrial A fly tied to imitate an insect that was not born in the water, such as a grasshopper, cricket, ant, or beetle.

Tippet Very thin, monofilament line added to the end of a leader to extend the length or to rebuild the leader after tippet has been used up tying knots or broken off.

Wader Belt A stretchable belt worn around the waist of waders, to keep the water out should the wearer slip and fall into the water.

Line Weight Fly line size by the weight of the first 30' of line. Weights from 1 light, to 15 heavy.

Weight Forward Fly line with more weight toward the front to assist in casting.

Wet Fly A fly fished below, or in the surface film of water.

Wild Fish born in the waters in which they are found, as opposed to fish stocked into their current waters.

Wooly Bugger A wet fly tied to give the impression of underwater food items of interest to fish.

"X" Ratings A system describing the approximate thickness of leaders and tippets. 010X (equaling .021 diameter at the tippet = large) down to 7X (equaling .004 diameter at the tippet = human hair size).

Definitions from Gary Graham and
The Easy Field Guide to Fly-Fishing Terms & Tips by David Phares.
For the complete list of terms, tips and some humor send $2.00 to: Primer
Publishers 5738 North Central Avenue Phoenix, Arizona 85012

No Nonsense Fly Fishing Knots

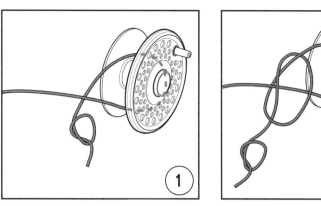

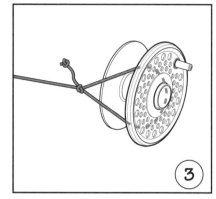

Arbor Knot Use this knot to attach backing to your fly reel. 75 yards of backing will be plenty for most waters.

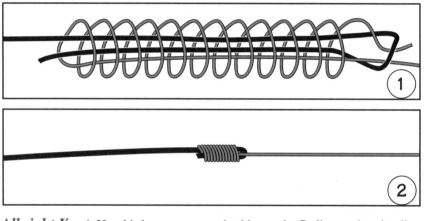

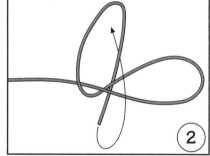

Albright Knot Use this knot to connect backing to the fly line or shooting line

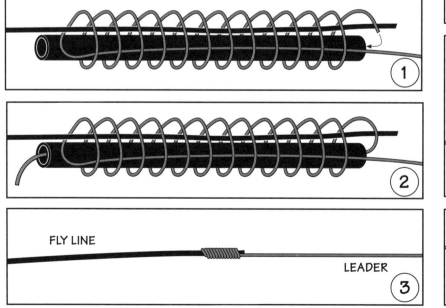

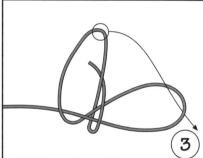

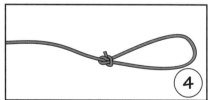

FLY LINE

LEADER

Nail Knot Use a nail, needle or a small tube to tie this knot, which connects the forward end of the fly line to the butt end of the leader. Follow this with a Perfection Loop, and you've got a permanent end loop that allows easy leader changes.

Perfection Loop Use this knot to create a loop in the butt end of the leader. You can easily "loop-to-loop" your leader to your fly line.

No Nonsense Fly Fishing Knots

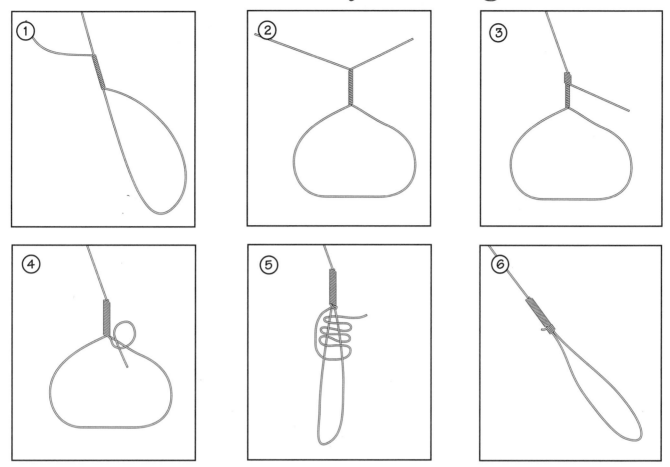

Bimini Twist Very important knot for building shock-absorbing leaders, and very difficult to tie. Nearly 100% knot strength.
1. Form loop and twist 20 times. **2.** Slip the loop over your knee and pull ends apart, forcing the twists together. **3.** Pull tag end at a right angle to the column of twists while pulling up on the standing end. Pull slightly downward on tag end and allow it to wrap around the column toward the loop. **4.** Continue to roll tag end around the column of twists until you reach the loop. Pinch the last wrap between fingers and make a half-hitch around one leg of the loop and pull tight. Remove loop from knee. **5.** Grab tag end and make 4 or 5 turns over both legs of the loop, wrapping backward toward the base of the loop. **6.** Pull and tighten slowly, causing the sprials to bunch up against base of loop. Trim tag end.

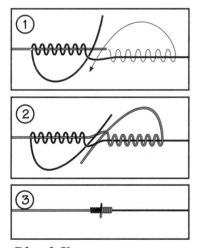

Blood Knot Use this knot to connect sections of leader material. To add a dropper, leave the heavier tag end long and attach fly.

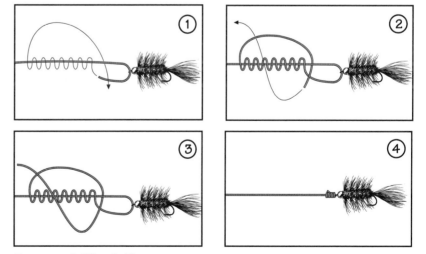

Improved Clinch Knot Use this knot to attach a fly to the end of the tippet.

Other
No Nonsense Guides

Glenn Tinnin's No Nonsense Guide To Fly Fishing In Arizona

Black River, Lees Ferry, Chevelon, Christmas Tree, Powell, and Lee Valley lakes, The Little Colorado River, Oak Creek and more!
ISBN #1-892469-02-2

If visiting the many scenic wonders of the Grand Canyon State, or moving there, bring your rod and this guide! Glenn Tinnin, outfitter at The Complete Fly Fisher in Scottsdale has explored Arizona's fly fishing waters for over 20 years. He explains where to go and how to fly fish mountain streams, lakes, bass waters, reservoirs and nearby saltwater fly fishing in Mexico.

Bob Zeller's No Nonsense Business Traveler's Guide To Fly Fishing The Western States

This seasoned road warrior reveals where one can fly fish within a two hour drive from every major airport in the western states.
ISBN #1-892469-01-4

Traveling on business (or for some other reason)? Turn drudgery into a fun fly fishing outing. Here's how to pack, what to tell the boss, and what to expect. Lots of detailed, two colored maps show where to go and how to get there.

With to-the-point facts and humor Bob's 30 years of fly fishing-while-on-the-road are your guide to exploring the outdoors, not just a hotel lobby or airport lounge.

Taylor Streit's No Nonsense Guide To Fly Fishing In New Mexico

The San Juan, Cimarron, Gila, Chama, Rio Grande, mountain lakes and more.
ISBN #0-9637256-6-1

The first all inclusive guide to the top fly fishing waters in the *Land of Enchantment*. Since 1970 Mr. Streit has been *THE* New Mexico fly fishing authority and #1 professional guide. He's also developed many fly patterns used throughout the region. Taylor owned the Taos Fly Shop for ten years and managed a bone fishing lodge in the Bahamas. He makes winter fly fishing pilgrimages to Argentina where he escorts fly fishers and explores.

Gary Graham's No Nonsense Guide To Fly Fishing Southern Baja

With this book you can fly to Baja, rent a car and go out on your own and find exciting saltwater fly fishing!
ISBN #1-892469-00-6

Mexico's Baja Peninsula is now one of the premier destinations for saltwater fly anglers. Here's the latest and best information from Baja fly fishing authority, Gary Graham. This Orvis endorsed guide has over 20 years of Baja fishing experience. He operates *Baja on the Fly*, a top guiding operation located in Baja's famed "East Cape" region.

Dave Stanley's No Nonsense Guide To Fly Fishing In Nevada

The Truckee, Walker, Carson, Eagle, Davis, Ruby, mountain lakes and more.
ISBN #0-9637256-2-9

Mr. Stanley is recognized nationwide as the most knowledgeable fly fisher and outdoorsman in the state of Nevada. He also travels throughout the west and other warm climes where he leads fly fishing excursions. He owns and operates the *Reno Fly Shop* and *River Outfitters* in Truckee.

The guide's talented coauthor, Jeff Cavender, is a Nevada native. Jeff teaches fly casting and tying. He's taught and guided all over Nevada and California during the past 30 + years. He also edits fly fishing guidebooks.

NO NONSENSE

FLY FISHING GUIDEBOOKS

Bill Mason's No Nonsense Guide To Fly Fishing In Idaho

The Henry's Fork, Salmon, Snake and Silver Creek plus 24 other waters.
ISBN #0-9637256-1-0

Mr. Mason penned the first fly fishing guidebook to Idaho in 1994. It was updated in 1996 and showcases Bill's 30 plus years of Idaho fly fishing experience.

Bill helped build a major outfitting operation at the Henry's Fork and helped open the first fly shop in Boise. In Sun Valley he developed the first fly fishing school and guiding program at Snug Fly Fishing. Bill eventually purchased the shop, renaming it Bill Mason Sun Valley Outfitters.

Jackson Streit's No Nonsense Guide To Fly Fishing In Colorado

The Colorado, Rio Grande, Platte, Gunnison, Mountain lakes and more.
ISBN #0-9637256-4-5

Mr. Streit fly fished Colorado for over 28 years and condensed this experience into a guidebook, published in 1995 and updated, improved and reprinted in 1997.

Jackson started the first guide service in the Breckenridge area and in 1985 he opened the region's first fly shop, The Mountain Angler, which he owns and manages.

Look for new No Nonsense Fly Fishing guides to other important regions!

Ken Hanley's No Nonsense Guide To Fly Fishing In Northern California

The "Sac", Hat Creek, Russian River, reservoirs, saltwater and bass on a fly.
ISBN #0-9637256-5-3

Mr. Hanley has fly fished nearly every water in N. California. While traveling the world and leading adventure expeditions he's caught over 50 species of gamefish. He's also written much on the subject including five other books. Ken also writes outdoor related pieces for a variety of publications.

Terry Barron's No Nonsense Guide To Fly Fishing Pyramid Lake

The Gem of the Desert is full of huge Lahontan Cutthroat trout.
ISBN #0-9637256-3-7

Mr. Barron is the Reno-area and Pyramid Lake fly fishing guru. He helped establish the Truckee River Fly Fishers Club and ties and works for the Reno Fly Shop.

Terry has recorded the pertinent information to fly fish the most outstanding trophy cutthroat fishery in the U.S. Where else can you get tired of catching 18-25" trout?

Harry Teel's No Nonsense Guide To Fly Fishing In Central & Southeastern Oregon

The Metolius, Deschutes, McKenzie, Owyhee, John Day and 35 other waters.
ISBN #0-9637256-9-6

Mr. Teel combined his 60 years of fly fishing into the first *No Nonsense* fly fishing guide. It was published in 1993 and updated, expanded and improved in 1998 by Jeff Perin. Jeff owns and operates the Fly Fisher's Place, the premier fly shop in Sisters, Oregon originally started by Mr. Teel.

Where No Nonsense Guides Come From

No Nonsense guidebooks give you a quick, clear, understanding of the essential information needed to fly fish a region's most outstanding waters. The authors are highly experienced and qualified local fly fishers. Maps are tidy versions of the authors sketches.

These guides are produced by the fly fishers, their friends, and spouses of fly fishers, at David Communications. The publisher is located in the tiny Western town of Sisters, Oregon, just a few miles from the Metolius River.

All who produce No Nonsense guides believe in providing top quality products at a reasonable price. We also believe all information should be verified. We never hesitate to go out, fly rod in hand, to verify the facts and figures that appear in the pages of these guides. The staff is committed to this research. It's dirty work, but we're glad to do it for you.

The layout, illustrations and maps in these books are the work of Pete Chadwell. As a fly fisherman, Pete is more than happy to apply his considerable drawing talents to things that live and float in and on water. His detailed maps are a testimony to his desire for accuracy and to get out and fly fish new waters.

No Nonsense fly fishing guides are edited by Jeff Cavender. This casting instructor, guide and author edits and writes fly fishing articles, books and guides. David Banks does the amateur editing.

Photo Credits

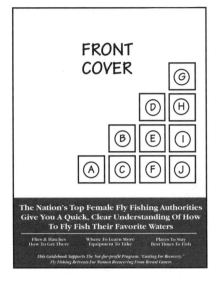

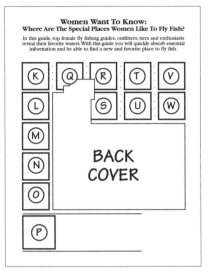

FRONT COVER, CLEARWATER RIVER
Photo By: Marty Downey

Ⓐ JANET DOWNEY
Photo By: Lefty Kreh

Ⓑ WANDA TAYLOR
Photo By: David S. Soliday

Ⓒ LORI-ANN MURPHY
Photo By: Greg Vondorsten

Ⓓ JOAN WULFF
Photo By: Tom Pero

Ⓔ FANNY KRIEGER
Photo Provided

Ⓕ NANCY MORRIS
Photo Provided

Ⓖ CECILIA "PUDGE" KLEINKAUF
Photo By: Michael DeYoung

Ⓗ MAGGIE MERRIMAN
Photo Provided

Ⓘ NANCY JOBE & SON
Photo Provided

Ⓙ SISTER CAROL ANNE CORLEY
Photo By: Char Maine Beleele

Ⓚ MARGOT PAGE
Photo Provided

Ⓛ LISA CUTTER
Photo Provided

Ⓜ JEAN WILLIAMS
Photo Provided

Ⓝ THREE FLY FISHERS
Photo Provided

Ⓞ JAN CRAWFORD
Photo Provided

Ⓟ YVONNE GRAHAM
Photo Provided

Ⓠ JOAN STOLIAR
Photo Provided

Ⓡ RAINY RIDING
Photo By: Fast Focus Productions

Ⓢ DOROTHY SCHRAMM
Photo Provided

Ⓣ PATTY REILLY
Photo Provided

Ⓤ NANCY ZAKON
Photo Provided

Ⓥ McKENZIE BANKS (Future Fly Fisher)
Photo By: Dad

Ⓦ MISA ISHAMURA
Photo Provided